GOD
SAVE THE
QUEEN!

BRITAIN IN
1952

Schweppshire Post

VOL. CICLXVIII No. 96   CIRENSCHWEPSTER, 1952.   SCHWEPPENCE

COUNCILLOR COLLIDES WITH COW

ESCAPES WITH SLIGHT ABRASIONS

Schwepton Mallet, Tuesday

A small automobile was the focus of what might have been an unpleasant event for Schweppshire this morning. Pedestrians were taken unaware when

Councillor Alfred Yoke, turning past Galway Mansions, found himself face to face with an un-guarded Shorthorn, which, but for Yoke's presence of mind, might have received serious injury.

POST has long campaigned for one way traffic in Waterworks Lane. Here, if further proof were needed, is further proof that yet another POST campaign should not be allowed to join the realm of lost causes.

Councillor Yoke (left). Cow (right)

Powers sign treaty

"A TURNING POINT" SAYS ENVOY
SCHWEPPSHIRE FIRM SUPPLIED BLOTTER

Where Schweppshire SPEAKS to the World

Our 2,000th Registered Reader will meet the Editors of 'POST'

Everyone in Cirenschwepster knows the POST offices at the corner of Groabham Gardens, spaciously design-ed to give pleasant working conditions to our eager staff. Triple fenestration allows maximum egress to light and air, and a lofty aspect overlooks one of Cirenschwepster's most teeming scenes.

Telephonic communica-tion puts POST within immediate reach of Schweppshire's farthest corners. A delivery van, on which we have first claims. *(TURN TO P. 4, COL. 6)*

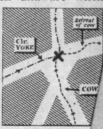

The Offices of POST (arrow), Visible in the picture:
1. *Home and Colonial Editor*
2. *City and Fashion Editor*
3. *Agricultural and Art Editor*
4. *Schweppshire Lad (Sport and Public Relations)*

AN ANNOUNCEMENT

The more than international interest aroused by the Guide to Schweppshire demands a response. We hope, during 1952, to be able to reprint pages from our daily organ, THE SCHWEPPSHIRE POST, thus vividly pin-pointing, uniquely, SCHWEPPSHIRE'S LIFE TO-DAY

... for ye that fare further, longer is the way ...

STREETCAR KIDNAPPED
in Hove, Pa.

SCHWEPPSHIRE VISITOR got off in time

J. Johns, our local apothecary, nearly had first-hand experience of gang warfare, when *(Turn to p. 2, col. 1)*

World Premiere
NEW FILM ACCLAIMED
Sehweppshire Man in charge of Buffet

I chanced on "Bandy" Rombold of Aden Gardens dealing out drinks smartly to a *(TURN TO P. 4. COL. 6)*

WEATHER FORECAST. GENERAL: *Dull inter-vals.* NORTH: *Dull all day.* SOUTH: *Intensely dull.* MIDDLE: *Schweppitome of dullness.*

Written by Stephen Potter · Drawn by Lewitt-Him

An unusual piece of publicity for Schweppes.

GOD
SAVE THE
QUEEN!

BRITAIN IN
1952

PETER STREET

SUTTON PUBLISHING

First Published in 2002 by
Sutton Publishing Limited · Phoenix Mill
Thrupp · Stroud · Gloucestershire ·GL5 2BU

Reprinted in 2002

British Library Cataloguing in Publication Data
A catalogue record for this book is available from the British Library

ISBN 0-7509-2796-8

Typeset in 10.5/13.5 Photina
Typesetting and origination by
Sutton Publishing Limited.
Printed in England by
J.H. Haynes & Co. Ltd, Sparkford.

To my mother and late father
who raised a son of 1952
and
Maria who married one

WITCHCRAFT LACE

in this year of grace

SUNDAY GRAPHIC

No. 1,923. February 17, 1952   (D)   A Kemsley Newspaper 2½d.

THE KING THE PEOPLE LOVED

THE QUEEN WHO IS OUR HOPE

We have said our last farewells to King George VI.   Let us remember him not in sadness, but in the spirit that he would himself have wished, putting grief behind us in the memory of his courage, his kindliness and his faith. Those virtues that we loved in him live on unconquerably in his daughter, our Queen.

The *Sunday Graphic*'s front page reflects the public mood perfectly.

CONTENTS

New Year's Eve celebrations in Trafalgar Square, 1950s.

ACKNOWLEDGEMENTS

This book would not have been possible without the help and patience of many people. These include family, friends and students who willingly gave their time to be questioned on life during and their reaction to the events of 1952. I would also like to thank the staff of University of London Library, Westminster Reference Library, Lord's Day Observance Society, Natural History Museum, Royal British Legion and the Royal Society for the Prevention of Cruelty to Animals for all the information which they made available. A special thanks also to Sutton Publishing (Christopher Feeney, Jane Crompton and Anne Bennett) for their support and guidance in bringing this idea to fruition.

Picture Research – Kate Middleton/Image Select International. All pictures, unless stated otherwise, courtesy of Topham Picturepoint.

ONE

Good Morning, 1952

Oh what a night! In Trafalgar Square the New Year had been seen in with bagpipes, fireworks, balloons, paper hats and rattles, while Piccadilly was where British and American servicemen chose to celebrate the occasion. In case things got out of hand, though, the police had surrounded and protected Eros. In the West End of London hotels and nightclubs were active and there were an estimated six thousand people at the annual Chelsea Arts Ball which took place at the Royal Albert Hall.

It was, however, already proving a prosperous new year for one group of gatecrashers. There were some uninvited guests at a party hosted by Princess Elizabeth's Private Secretary in Hampstead. Thieves used a ladder left by workmen to gain entry through an open window and stole eleven fur coats (valued between £3,000 and £4,000) belonging to guests. Among those who were robbed amid all the noise of celebration was Miss Clarissa Churchill, a niece of the prime minister.

In a rather more restrained way St Paul's Cathedral, its dome and cross made all the more glorious by floodlighting, held a Watch-Night service to mark the arrival of 1952. The Watch-Night service held at Wesley's Chapel in the neighbouring City Road was transmitted live to the Methodist Church in Redhill, Surrey. Among those in that congregation was the prominent Methodist and British film mogul, J. Arthur Rank.

It was generally considered to have been a quiet Hogmanay in Scotland. Perhaps because of the weather (it was sleeting), there were fewer at the traditional meeting place of the old toll booth, Glasgow Cross. In the Lake District, though, many supported the night rambles there, with some even managing to climb the snow-covered peaks before midnight.

But for many people it was enough to 'see in the New Year' by staying up until midnight and then proposing a family toast, finishing up any alcohol that had been bought in especially for the Christmas period. Except for 'medicinal purposes', for various reasons fewer people had 'drink' in the home throughout the year.

An orderly queue of bicycles. The absence of other traffic is quite striking to twenty-first century eyes.

Generally speaking alcohol was bought by men from off-licences or specialist outlets rather than by women as part of general shopping. Few were yet able to enjoy the delights of duty free. Some might also have observed the occasion in another way – formally admitting the New Year by opening the front door and letting the old one out by the back. There would be friendly greetings to neighbours, similarly standing at their front doors, and many hoping (seriously or otherwise) that a dark-haired man would be the first to cross the threshold and bring luck to all within during the coming year.

Then it was time for bed. Celebrations had to be short-lived for most people, as Tuesday 1 January 1952 was a working day in England and Wales (but not in Scotland). By early morning many were already making their way to factory, mill, office or shop. This was still the age

when many walked, cycled or used public transport to reach their place of work – some perhaps taking advantage of the cheaper early morning (workmen's) fares where these were offered. The only form of personal transport used in significant numbers was the bicycle. Several hundred workers might arrive in this way at the factory entrance. Apparent chaos and real *bonhomie* prevailed as people struggled to find a bicycle rack, perhaps clock on and be ready for the day ahead.

The first day of a C&A sale in the 1950s.

Others meantime had also got up early – and gone shopping. On New Year's Day the January sales had started in earnest throughout the country. Among those to benefit before making any purchases were people outside the Co-operative Society store in Nottingham. There the management arranged for the first fifty people in the queue to be presented with rum and coffee at 7am.

FRONT-PAGE NEWS

Others might travel in a more leisurely manner to their place of work. This was still the age of the 'city gent' complete with bowler hat, umbrella and *The Times*. Priced 3*d* (it was to be increased to 4*d* in February, its first increase since 1941), the newspaper still carried advertisements on the front page. This was a conscious recognition that it (like other newspapers) was dependent on advertising (essentially classified) to continue in existence. The cover price made a relatively small contribution to revenue. That morning, as every morning, the first entries were births, marriages, anniversaries and deaths. The entries on 1 January included a notice marking the sixtieth wedding anniversary of George Constance and Edith Ward. They had been married at the beginning of 1892 by Canon Thompson at the parish church of Aldeburgh and were still living there. Among the death notices was that of Mary, widow of Colonel Charles Murray Alexander of Pomeroy House, Pomeroy, Co. Tyrone. She was in her ninety-fourth year and had therefore witnessed considerable change, especially in Ireland. Born a dozen years after the Great Famine she had lived to see the larger part of the island proclaimed a republic.

Should readers be contemplating a change of employment there was a vacancy (only men were invited to apply) for the position of Director General of the Advertising Association. The annual salary was £2,000. Other job opportunities in that day's *Times* included one for a public schoolboy, aged between fifteen and eighteen, to train for the hotel business. The Civil Service was inviting applications from those aged between fifteen and twenty who wished to become clerical staff (Grade II). Although examinations had to be sat, these required 'no special preparation' as they were 'simple tests in common sense, accuracy and arithmetic'. Finally, for anyone wanting to get away from it all for this year there were fellowships (£450) and scholarships (£382) on offer from the British Institute of Archaeology at Ankara. Twelve copies of the application and twelve copies of the testimonials, however, had to be submitted!

The classified advertisements also included one from a regular army lieutenant-colonel bachelor who sought accommodation within ten minutes' walk of Horse Guards Parade. He was willing to pay up to 8 guineas a week for a 'home from home' provided it offered 'contentment'. There was a country vicar looking for a '14 horse-power' car, and he was willing to pay up to £450. There was also a church cleaning company promoting itself under the heading 'talking miracles'. This argued that 'cleanliness is a form of godliness' and suggested that unless the building was clean, a church's 'customers' (the advertisement's description) might not return.

Bodily needs were also met. Featured on the front page were a new plucked otter coat (£160), a four-skin sable tie (£80) and 'massage'

Model in Mink

Harrods

Winston Churchill seen
addressing a joint session of
Congress in Washington DC,
1952.

foam from 'Ray aids' in Baron's Court, London. Alcoholic craving
could be stopped, it was claimed, by using Turvy Tonic and colds
avoided by carrying Besorbon Medicinal Snuff.

NEWLY HONOURED

The New Year's Honours were listed in full in that morning's press.
It was Winston Churchill's first such peacetime list and included
hereditary peerages (life peerages did not exist) and baronetcies.
Among those honoured were Sir John Anderson (Viscount
Waverley), Sir Archibald Sinclair (Viscount Thurso) and Brendan
Bracken (Viscount Bracken). Earl Winterton, an Irish peer who had
sat in the House of Commons from 1904 to 1951, was created a Baron
of the United Kingdom.

Knighthoods were bestowed on Hugh Casson, Director of
Architecture for the Festival of Britain, which had taken place the
previous summer and had attracted eight and a half million visitors.
Also honoured in this way were Allen Lane, the founder of Penguin
Books, and John Rothenstein, the Director and Keeper of the Tate

TOP FILMS OF THE YEAR

High Noon (Fred Zinnemann; Gary Cooper, Grace Kelly, Ian MacDonald, Lloyd Bridges, Thomas Mitchell)

The Quiet Man (John Ford; John Wayne, Maureen O'Hara, Barry Fitzgerald, Victor McLaglen)

The Bad and the Beautiful (Vincente Minnelli; Kirk Douglas, Lana Turner, Walter Pidgeon, Dick Powell)

The Greatest Show on Earth (Cecil B. DeMille; Charlton Heston, Dorothy Lamour, Cornel Wilde)

Gallery. In the entertainment world Anna Neagle and Flora Robson were both honoured by being made Commanders of the British Empire. Anna Neagle, married to the film producer Herbert Wilcox, had made her name playing various historical figures, most famously Queen Victoria. In 1951 Wilcox had produced *The Lady with a Lamp*, in which she had starred as Florence Nightingale.

Flora Robson already had over twenty years' experience as a film actress by 1952. Probably her most celebrated work to date was in *Fire over England* (1936, in which she played Queen Elizabeth) and *Black Narcissus* (1946). In 1952 she made *The Tall Headlines*, which concerned the impact on the family when the eldest son was executed for murder. This won relatively little critical success.

The grouping of awards revealed the continuing relationship between Honours and Empire, with the Colonial Office, Commonwealth Relations Office and Foreign Office each having its own list, as did some overseas territories such as Australia and New Zealand. There were also awards for service in the ongoing Korean War.

'LEVELLING DOWN IN EDUCATION'

Educational matters featured prominently on that first day of 1952. Miss G.M.B. Williams, in her presidential address the previous day to the annual meeting of the Association of Assistant Mistresses in Secondary Schools, had expressed concern over 'levelling down in education'. She supported the recent (1944) Education Act which, primarily through grammar schools and secondary modern schools, offered secondary education for all. But she remained anxious over how the system was developing, in particular that equality of education under that system was too often being interpreted as 'indiscriminate equalising' of education. She believed that such an approach harmed the gifted child in denying him or her – regardless of class or economic background – the highest type of education on offer. The bright pupil, Miss Williams argued, was not a unit in a convoy travelling at the speed of the slowest ship, and she pleaded for recognition of 'the aristocracy of talent'.

Miss Williams' speech also drew attention to the deterioration in the supply of 'gifted grammar school' teachers and the danger of teaching becoming a 'minor administrative job and cramped by all kinds of petty restrictions, official directives and official safeguards'. She saw teaching as a creative art: if the nation wanted good teachers then they should be given the freedom to create and experiment. The continuing loss of independence in schools could eventually reduce staff to the level of 'operatives "minding" a machine in an increasingly mechanised educational factory'.

SCHOOLBOYS' OWN EXHIBITION

Currently taking place at the Horticultural Halls, Westminster, this exhibition (despite its name) was for girls as well as boys. It had been opened by Peter Brough the ventriloquist with his celebrated dummy Archie Andrews and was a recruitment fair for those fifteen-year-olds about to leave school. Among those represented were the three armed services. Both sexes had the opportunity to jump from a full-size army parachute training tower to the landing mats some 36 feet below. The girls (described as 'young Amazons') wore khaki parachute crash helmets. There was also the chance to bomb a submarine.

British Railways also took part and their electrically operated model railway with some 500 feet of track and the new BR standard locomotives was particularly popular. Another transport challenge was to ride a TT (Tourist Trophy) racing motorcycle. The course unfolded on a screen and equated to travelling at 70 mph. But road safety was not neglected as there were people on hand to explain the recent innovation of the zebra crossing.

NEWS IN BRIEF

Peter Brough, the radio ventriloquist, and his puppet Archie Andrews.

Among the domestic stories of the day was a report on the transfer of the Crystal Palace site in south London from the Crystal Palace Trust to the London County Council (LCC). This had been marked the day before with a lunch at the London Guildhall. Speakers from the Trust, the LCC and others all hoped that 'when conditions permitted', the site would be restored to its former glories and that the successor Crystal Palace (that of 1851, built to house the Great Exhibition, was destroyed by fire in 1936) would become a place for education and recreation, but that it might promote industry, commerce and art as well.

Meanwhile, the 1951 Festival of Britain, which had taken place in part to celebrate the centenary of the Great Exhibition, was under attack. Its former Director of Architecture Hugh Casson, looking back on the event, was reported to have said that the Dome of

Discovery was not so adventurous as the organisers thought it would be. Intended to be visualised as a great empty brain, it was more murkiness than mystery, creating an environment that oppressed rather than inspired.

In terms of leisure pursuits, there was a report that Mr Tompkins of Woburn, Bedfordshire, hoped to go fox hunting that day. Aged eighty, he had been riding since January 1882. Other country matters included an outbreak of foot and mouth disease near Lowestoft in Suffolk, and since 21 December ninety-six cases of salmonella poisoning had been reported in the Towcester area of Northamptonshire. Finally readers were told that the inquest had opened the previous day in Hammersmith, London, on the 'wall of death' motor cyclist who had died from injuries suffered while performing at Bertram Mills' Circus at Olympia.

TUNING IN

The newspaper was no longer the only national source of information and entertainment. Radio broadcasting had begun in the early 1920s and the single television service had been re-established by the British Broadcasting Corporation in June 1946. But, while radio had penetrated nearly every home by 1952, television was only in a small minority of households in that year.

There were three BBC radio stations in 1952 – the Home Service, the Light Programme and the Third Programme. On 1 January the Home Service broadcast for over sixteen hours (6.30am to 11pm), the Light for slightly less (fifteen hours; beginning and ending later) while the Third was on air in the evening only.

Most of the Home Service programmes for the day comprised music, news/weather, variety and religion. The station opened with music and included *Music While You Work* (simultaneously broadcast on the Light Programme), *Have a Go*, *Workers' Playtime*, *Evensong* (3pm) and the very popular *Children's Hour*. Among the evening broadcasts were *Cinderella* and a play. The Light Programme offered *Mrs Dale's Diary* (twice – morning and afternoon), *Listen with Mother*, another instalment of *Music While You Work* and at 6.45pm *The Archers*. Later that evening were the programmes *Take It From Here* and *Argument*. The latter was a discussion between William Deedes and (as then billed) Anthony Wedgwood Benn. *Book at Bedtime* was broadcast at 11pm. Music, perhaps understandably, dominated the Third Programme's fare, and featured works by Dvorak, Bach (*Christmas Oratorio*) and Paganini. But there was also a dramatised version of Thomas Peacock's novel *Crotchet Castle*.

William Deedes.

Ostensibly there were over seven hours of television on New Year's Day, lasting from 3pm until 10.25pm. But there were breaks between programmes and sometimes (deliberately) sound only. The features broadcast on 1 January included the children's regular programme *Andy Pandy* in the afternoon. But there were specials too – *Aladdin* in the early evening and a play with Mary Jerrold, Griffith Jones and Anthony Ireland entitled *For Better or Worse*.

Richard Dimbleby, the best-known radio voice of the 1950s, recording *Down Your Way* at the Bath and Wessex Orthopaedic Hospital in Bath.

LONDON THEATRE

Those working in, living in or able to travel to the capital enjoyed a wide choice of live entertainment that night – from the revue at the Windmill (which in relation to its wartime service proudly, if slightly misleadingly, boasted 'we never closed') to *Il Trovatore* at Covent Garden conducted by Capuana. The (future Royal) Festival Hall offered Christmas ballet with seats priced from 12*s* 6*d* to 3*s* 6*d*. Matinee tickets for children were half price.

The plays/actors in the capital included Eric Portman in *Moment of Truth* by Peter Ustinov, Jack Hulbert in *White Sheep of the Family* by Ian Hay, and John Mills in *Figure of Fun*. According to the publicity, though, London's wittiest comedy was *To Dorothy a Son*, which starred Richard Attenborough and Sheila Sim. *Blue for a Boy* with Fred Emney and Richard Hearne (the future 'Mr Pastry') and *Waters of the Moon* (Sybil Thorndike, Kathleen Harrison and Wendy Hiller) were also in performance, as were *Kiss Me Kate* and *The Hollow* by Agatha Christie; *The Mousetrap* did not open until later in 1952.

Also on stage at this time were George Formby and Joyce Grenfell. There was *Humpty Dumpty* at the Palladium with Noele Gordon, Terry-Thomas and Jean Bayless and *Aladdin* at the London Casino. The cast here included the Tiller Girls; Julie Andrews played the Prince. Musicals included Mary Martin in *South Pacific* at Drury Lane, *Puss in Boots* at the Empress Hall and *Robinson Crusoe* on ice at the Empire Pool, which had a cast of 200. On the more serious side there was Emlyn Williams as Charles Dickens and Yvonne Arnaud in Jean Anouilh's *Colombe*. Finally, in complete contrast, there were *Encore des Folies* (the second year of a Folies Bergère production), a stage version of Walt Disney's *Snow White* and *Archie Andrews' Christmas Party*.

Programme for *South Pacific*: it cost sixpence!

BRITAIN IN 1952: ANALYSIS OF A NATION

Sunday 8 April 1951 had seen the first census in Britain for twenty years. The UK population totalled some 50,210,000, with England and Wales accounting for most of it (over 87 per cent). At 550 people per square mile in Britain as a whole, this area was one of the most densely populated in the world and the figure was continuing to rise. It was also one of the most heavily urbanised areas in the world. Greater London had over 8.3 million people while more than a million lived in each of Birmingham and Glasgow. Altogether there were twenty cities with a population of over 200,000. Medium towns (50,000–100,000) were growing fastest, with some of the small towns beginning to decline. Garden Cities, established earlier in the twentieth century, and New Towns such as Stevenage, created in the postwar era, were continuing to expand.

The population growth was in part the result of higher birth rates – 1947 had seen the highest birth rate since 1921. Although in subsequent years they were to be progressively lower, these were still higher than pre-war figures and together formed part of the postwar baby boom, generally dated to 1945–55. Most families in mid-century, however, had only one or two children.

The population was also rising because people were living longer and there was a net gain from migration. Most of those leaving the UK headed for Commonwealth countries – Australia, Canada, New Zealand and South Africa. But the USA was also popular. The movement into Britain was mainly a mix of people from all over the Empire and Commonwealth. Following the 1948 Nationality Act there were no restrictions on such movement, and settlement was to some extent encouraged because of labour shortages.

A group of West Indians arrive in Southampton.

About two-thirds of the population were of working age (fifteen to sixty-four), with about a fifth under fifteen and a tenth over sixty-five. There were slightly more females than males, a predominance which increased with age. Women outnumbered men from adolescence and there were nearly 50 per cent more women than men aged seventy plus. Life expectancy in 1952 was sixty-six for men and almost seventy for women. The main natural causes of death were cancer, coronary and heart disease, bronchitis, pneumonia and tuberculosis. Most violent deaths were the result of accidents. There were more suicides than motor vehicle deaths. Some three hundred people in 1952 were either murdered or died in action.

Though English was the language of Britain, Welsh was spoken by a quarter of the population in the Principality. It was also estimated that some 100,000 people spoke Gaelic, with a particularly strong presence in Ross and Cromarty, Inverness, Argyll and Lanark. But fewer than 2,700 spoke Gaelic only. Few now spoke the Manx and Cornish varieties of Celtic, though Irish Gaelic in Northern Ireland and French in the Channel Islands continued to be used.

The country was governed by the Conservatives. They had been returned to office in October 1951, following six years of Labour government. The prime minister, Churchill, was seventy-seven years old and this was to be his only peacetime government. He was to be succeeded by Sir Anthony Eden in 1955. The newness of the government was reflected in the unveiling of the wax models of the Cabinet at Madame Tussaud's in early January 1952. Those featured in addition to Churchill included Anthony Eden (Foreign Secretary), R.A. ('Rab') Butler (Chancellor of the Exchequer) and Harold Macmillan (Minister for Housing).

Peter Robinson's store in Cheltenham experiments with self-service. One rack is marked 'Utility Coats', although the war had been over for six years.

The Second World War had had a massive adverse impact on Britain's financial and trading position, primarily because of the loss of some overseas assets, new overseas debts and reduced exports. Industry had had to change over from war to peacetime output. An exhibition had been held in the autumn of 1946 called 'Britain Can Make It'. Designed by the young Scottish architect Basil Spence (who went on to win the competition for Coventry Cathedral in 1951), it showed how industry had responded to the challenge. But given the enforced priority of export markets, many thought 'Britain Can't Have It' would have been a more accurate title for the exhibition.

Socially, too, the aftermath of war was still very real in 1952. Many areas still bore witness to the blitz with the burnt-out shells of homes, churches and local facilities all too evident. Similarly rationing and identity cards were still in force when the year began. But there were to be changes in both. Some items came off rationing in 1952 and the identity card was abolished in February although its number was not discarded. This now became the person's National Health Service number. Numbers were also provided for babies and others who had not been part of the registration system.

Governing Britain

The government was only a few months old when 1952 began. The general election held in the previous October had seen the return of a purely Conservative government for the first time in almost thirty years. It was also the first time the Conservatives had been returned to power since the establishment of one person one vote in Britain. The Representation of the People Act (1948) had abolished the business and university vote. Plural voting, however, continued to feature in Northern Ireland elections.

The 1951 election marked the end of six years of Labour government and overturned the landslide majority (146 seats) which that party had secured in 1945. In the intervening period the first majority Labour government had achieved significant changes both in the nature of the economy and in the provision of social security. To the years 1945–51 belong the nationalisation of the Bank of England, the coal industry, civil aviation, electricity (previously it had been just the generation of electricity), railways, canals, gas, iron and steel. This period also saw the establishment of non-contributory family allowances, the ending of the last remnants of the Poor Law system with consequent improvements in unemployment pay and sick benefits, and perhaps most importantly the birth of the National Health Service. The mixed economy and the welfare provision which the Conservatives inherited in 1951 were to remain largely unchanged for the next thirty years.

During its period of office, 1945–51, the Labour government did not lose a single by-election. Even so, it was only returned with an overall majority of six MPs in February 1950. Consequently (and rightly) many expected that a further general election would be called before long. Even so, this was the first parliament, however brief, for such future leading Conservatives as Edward Heath, Reginald Maudling, Iain Macleod, Enoch Powell and Christopher Soames. Similarly on the Labour side it was the first parliament for

Jo Grimond.

Tony Crosland and Roy Jenkins. Joseph ('Jo') Grimond became a Liberal MP for the first time.

The second Attlee administration ended abruptly. King George VI, who was to begin a six-month tour of the Commonwealth at the start of 1952, wrote to Attlee on 1 September expressing his anxiety about being out of the country for so long while the political situation was uncertain. The prime minister did not want to worry him and, without consulting Cabinet colleagues, asked for a dissolution on 19 September 1951. He announced the general election on the radio in a brief statement before the 9pm news the same day. This was the first time a prime minister had informed the nation of an election this way. Previously a statement had been made to parliament or issued to the press from 10 Downing Street. But no one seems to have objected.

Mr Attlee explained that parliament was to be dissolved on 5 October and that the election was to take place on 25 October. Thus two and a half weeks were to elapse between his announcement and the formal start of the general election campaign. Such longer notice was in contrast to the interwar period and indicative of the greater preparations which fighting an election campaign now entailed. This timetable also favoured Labour as it enabled the party to launch its campaign at the annual conference (1 October) and compelled the Conservatives to cancel their conference which was to have been held later in October. Similarly the Liberals were also forced to cancel their assembly (25–7 October).

GOD, THE KING AND THE CONSTITUTION

Despite the advance notice of the general election, there were few overt signs of significant political activity in the period before the dissolution. This was partly because the parties did not wish to tire party workers or to bore the electorate. But there was also the question of the king's illness. A few days after Mr Attlee's announce-ment on 23 September George VI underwent a lung operation at Buckingham Palace. Its seriousness led to some looking up the Meeting of Parliament Act (1797). Under that act, in the event of the demise of the sovereign between the dissolution of one parliament and the meeting of the next, the election becomes void and the old parliament reassembles. Therefore if the king had died after the general election but before the MPs met, Labour (in law) could have continued to govern, whatever the result.

On Thursday 4 October a pre-election service was held in St Paul's Cathedral, attended by leaders of all parties. Similar services were held in several constituencies and were seen as an appropriate

Clement Attlee.

occasion for a civilised and amiable opening to the campaign. After the service in St Paul's, parliament assembled for formal prorogation, preceded by brief and loyal speeches about the king's condition and hopes for his continued recovery. MPs then filed past the Speaker who was retiring at this election. Clifton Brown (Conservative) had been Speaker since 1943. Parliament was dissolved by royal proclamation the following day.

THE CANDIDATES

Nominations closed on 15 October. There were 1,376 candidates, fewer than in 1950. Each candidate was required to pay a deposit (£150). This amount had remained unchanged since it was first introduced in 1918. It was not returned (thereby becoming a lost deposit) if the candidate secured less than one-eighth of the total votes cast. The Communists fielded ten candidates, only one of whom stood in a Conservative-held seat (Mr Churchill's). The Independent Labour Party (forerunner of and founder member of the Labour Party) had three candidates. The Scottish National Party fought two seats, the Welsh Nationalists four. The latter had decided not to contest any constituencies where the existing MP or another candidate supported self-government for Wales. This benefited the Liberals most as they favoured parliaments for both Wales and

M.J. Rantzen, Conservative candidate for Hayes and Harlington in the 1951 election, campaigning from a caravan fitted with electric lighting, telephones and loudspeakers!

Scotland. Of the six seats won by the Liberal Party in the 1951 general election, three were in Wales and one in Scotland.

The Conservatives did not contest the three Welsh seats held by the Liberals nor five other constituencies elsewhere in Great Britain, and when they issued their list of prospective candidates they included the Liberals in all the Conservative-uncontested seats. This caused quite a furore on the part of the Liberals and a revised list was later published with the Liberal candidates in question now featuring in an appendix. The Liberal Party itself put up 109 candidates (leading subsequently to sixty-six lost deposits), while the Labour and Conservative Parties (including the National Liberal and Conservative Party) each fielded 617 candidates. This meant that in most constituencies it was a straight fight between the two major parties. Labour lost only one deposit in 1951.

THE CAMPAIGN

Labour entered the election trailing in the opinion polls but argued that if the Conservatives (led by Churchill) were to win, unemployment would rise, the Welfare State would be dismantled and war would be a real possibility. This last concern led to one leaflet proclaiming 'Vote Tory and reach for a rifle, Vote Labour and reach old age'; another slogan was 'Welfare with Labour or Warfare with the Tories'. Similarly, the *Daily Mirror*'s election day headline read 'Whose Finger on the Trigger?', a second attempt to portray Churchill as a warmonger. Churchill at once brought a legal action against the newspaper, its owners and editors. The prime minister won, the paper offering to pay costs and to give money to a charity nominated by him. But newspapers were not the only medium available to the electorate.

TELEVISION AND POLITICS

Television began broadcasting at the end of the 1920s. Ramsay MacDonald, the first Labour Prime Minister, had a set installed in 10 Downing Street in 1930. But little political use was made of this medium, given its small audience and limited reception area. Only once in the first three years of BBC television (1936–9) did a prime minister appear on television. This was Neville Chamberlain at Heston aerodrome, following his return from meeting Hitler in Munich in September 1938. Television was closed down from 1939 until 1946. Both Attlee and Churchill refused the BBC's offer of a political broadcast during the 1950 general election, in part because it would reach such a small audience. Political broadcasts on radio had begun in the 1930s and were still deemed to be sufficient. Subsequently the Conservatives appointed their first Head of Broadcasting – John Profumo, who in the early 1960s was to be the subject of the first major political scandal covered by television.

There were, however, political broadcasts on television during the October 1951 general election although neither news bulletins nor the main current affairs programme, *In the News*, carried coverage of the campaign. The first political broadcast was given by the Liberals. Viscount Samuel (first elected to parliament in 1902) read from a script for fifteen minutes, rarely looked at the camera, overran and was cut off in mid-sentence when he mistakenly gave the pre-arranged signal to show that he had finished! In contrast the Conservatives' broadcast was given by the suave Anthony Eden and took the form of a 'spontaneous' interview with another well-known figure, Leslie Mitchell. The broadcast included graphics purporting to illustrate increases in the cost of living. Christopher Mayhew gave the Labour broadcast. He also used graphs and showed how, with two such visual aids, identical data could be portrayed differently and provocatively. His third was an 'honest man's' graph which showed how the curve of increased prices had been flattening out until the outbreak of the Korean War (1950) had sent it soaring again. 'Crippen', he ended, 'was the first criminal to be caught by wireless; the Conservative Central Office are the first criminals to be caught by television.'

Anthony Eden.

Leslie Mitchell.

RADIO AND THE ELECTION

Despite its use, television could only reach a small audience whereas that for radio was (potentially) huge. Political broadcasts were normally transmitted at 9.15pm. According to the BBC's Audience Research Department, Labour speakers drew a smaller audience (33 per cent) than the Conservatives (40 per cent) and figures were down for both parties in comparison to February 1950. This could reflect the 'captive' audience in the depth of winter as much as declining interest in politics. Furthermore it was also argued that people were more likely to listen to those speaking for the party which they supported than to their opponents. Finally the Conservative audience was also thought to be bigger because political broadcasts, deemed to be serious listening, would attract the middle class and older people. Both such groups were more likely to vote for the Conservative Party.

THE OUTCOME OF THE ELECTION

The electorate totalled 34,645,573 and the turn-out was 82.5 per cent. This was slightly down on that of 1950 (84 per cent). The Labour vote was higher than in 1950 and more than the Conservative vote in 1951 itself, representing the largest number of votes ever cast for a British political party. The Conservative victory in part was attributed to fewer Liberal candidates than in the previous election. Most of the voters on that occasion now chose to support the Conservative cause where no Liberal was standing.

In comparison with the 1950 general election, there was an overall swing of 4.5 per cent to the Conservatives and 2.4 per cent to Labour, with a swing away from the Liberals of 6.6 per cent. The average error of polling organisations in predicting the vote of the two main parties was between 1.7 and 3.9 per cent.

Among the defeated candidates in 1951 were the Liberals Lady Violet Bonham-Carter and Lady Megan Lloyd-George and the Conservative candidate (and son of the prime minister) Randolph Churchill. He lost in a straight fight against Michael Foot at Plymouth Devonport. Two of Churchill's sons-in-law (Christopher Soames and Duncan Sandys) were re-elected. This was the first full parliament for, among others, Sir Edward Boyle and Anthony Barber (Conservatives and future ministers). Tony Benn (Labour) also became an MP for the first time.

CHURCHILL'S CABINET

Having fought (and won) his fourteenth general election, Churchill set about forming his administration. The details which follow relate to key office holders from then until the end of 1952.

Party	Total Votes	MPs Elected	Candidates	Unopposed Returns	% Share of Total Vote
Conservative	13,717,538	321	617	4	48.0
Liberal	730,556	6	109	nil	2.5
Labour	13,948,605	295	617	nil	48.8
Communist	21,640	nil	10	nil	0.1
Others	177,329	3	23	nil	0.6
Total	28,595,668	625	1,376	4	100

Churchill held the positions of Prime Minister and First Lord of the Treasury and was also Minister of Defence. But from 1 March 1952 Earl Alexander of Tunis was appointed to this last position. The Foreign Secretary was Anthony Eden (the third time he had been appointed to this post since 1935). Other Cabinet appointments included R.A. ('Rab') Butler as Chancellor of the Exchequer and Sir David Maxwell-Fyfe as Home Secretary. The latter was also Minister for Welsh Affairs. This meant that Wales, although unlike Scotland still without its own Secretary of State, was now for the first time directly represented in Cabinet. Peter Thorneycroft was made President of the Board of Trade. Walter Monckton was Minister of Labour and National Service (the term for conscription). In order for the government to develop a neutral image between labour and capital, Monckton was banned from attending Conservative Party conferences. Lord Cherwell (nicknamed 'The Prof' and a great personal friend of Churchill's) was given a roving commission as Paymaster-General.

Churchill also appointed three 'Overlords' – Lord Leathers as Minister for Co-ordination of Transport, Fuel and Power, Lord Woolton (of 'pie' fame) as Lord President of the Council and Lord Salisbury as Lord Privy Seal. Both the Colonies (Oliver Lyttelton) and the Commonwealth (Lord Ismay, followed by two others within little more than a year) each had their own Secretary of State in the Cabinet. They were in addition to the Foreign Secretary. In contrast, the Ministries of Health (once it had passed from Harry Crookshank to Iain Macleod in May 1952), Food and Education were all outside the Cabinet in 1952. Clement Davies, the leader of the Liberal Party, was offered the prospect of a Conservative–Liberal coalition and the post of Minister of Education. He was eager to accept but he was persuaded by other party members, notably Viscount Samuel and Megan Lloyd-George, to decline. Thereupon the Conservative Walter Elliot was telephoned to be asked if he would become Minister for Education. But he was not at home. Consequently the appointment went to Florence Horsborough, who subsequently became the first woman to sit in a Conservative Cabinet.

Clement Davies.

As regards future Conservative leaders, Anthony Eden (regarded by Churchill and others as his successor since the war years) was in the Cabinet, Harold Macmillan was appointed Minister of Housing and Local Government (with Ernest Marples as his Parliamentary Secretary); Lord (later Sir Alec Douglas-) Home was at the Scottish Office while Edward Heath joined the Whips Office. Margaret Thatcher, although a parliamentary candidate in the 1951 election, was not successful on that occasion.

THE HOUSE OF LORDS

Amid some controversy, Churchill made use of the second chamber and some important figures in his administration, notably the Minister of Defence, were there for much or all of 1952. The House of Lords at this time had fewer than 850 members, most of whom were hereditary peers – a group which included a specified number from Scotland (sixteen) and Ireland (five). There were also Peers of the Blood, twenty-six Anglican bishops and archbishops and several law lords. Hereditary peerages continued to be created at this time by both Labour and Conservative administrations, together with advances in rank. Other than for law lords, life peerages did not yet exist. Furthermore it was not possible to disclaim an hereditary peerage.

Miss Margaret Roberts campaigning in Dartford. Described as the best looking of the Conservative women candidates she was also said to be reading for the Bar in her spare time. Here she is speaking to Mr Evans, a local chimney-sweep.

The Irish and Scottish peers were elected by their fellow peers from the territories concerned. Those who were not so elected could stand for the Commons. No women were allowed to sit in this House.

The Lords had only recently moved back to their own chamber. Following the destruction of the House of Commons in the air raid of 10 May 1941 (the first anniversary of – but unconnected with – Churchill's accession to the wartime premiership), the Lords gave up its chamber to the Other House and the Robing Room was adapted for the Lords' use. With the rebuilding of the Commons completed, the Lords returned to their own chamber on 29 May 1951.

The members were predominantly Conservative but a convention had recently been established whereby the Lords did not block manifesto commitments of the governing party. Furthermore, the Parliament Act (1949) had reduced the House of Lords' delaying powers for non-money bills to two sessions and one year. Money bills, designated as such by the Speaker and which most significantly included the Budget, could be amended but not held back by the Lords. The royal assent was required to complete the legislative process but this had not been refused since the early eighteenth century.

THE CIVIL SERVICE

At the start of 1952 there were some 688,435 non-industrial civil servants. These included post office workers as well as those employed by government departments. Partly in response to the economic situation, the total number was reduced by about 15,000 during the course of the year. Civil service pensions were not index-linked to increases in the cost of living but legislation was passed at this time to reduce the hardship experienced by some retired employees. This had been caused by inflation since 1947. Among those to benefit were local authority staff, teachers, police and former employees of certain friendly and provident societies.

Although the bar on the employment of married women civil servants had been removed in 1946, there was still unequal pay. Resolutions seeking to end this situation had been passed by the House of Commons in 1920 and 1936. But these acknowledged that implementation of the change was dependent on the right economic circumstances, and these had yet to materialise. Equal pay for civil servants had featured in the Conservative Party manifesto for the 1950 general election. But, echoing the then Labour Chancellor's (Gaitskell's) opposition to the move in 1951, the Treasury in 1952 would still not agree to the change. Butler, his successor, was not to defeat this view until 1954. Equal pay for government employees began at the start of the following year.

Civil servants at work.

Civil Service unions had been allowed to resume party affiliation in 1946, but in 1949 the government had banned communists and fascists from any work deemed vital to the security of the state. This policy was continued under Churchill. In January 1952 further security procedures were brought in for staff employed on exceptionally secret work, including any with access to classified atomic energy information.

THE NEW SPEAKER

The new House of Commons assembled on 1 November 1951 and chose a new Speaker under the auspices of the father of the house, Sir Hugh O'Neill, who had first been elected just before the First World War. W.S. ('Shakes') Morrison, a Conservative, was successful in the first challenge for the post since 1895. He held the post until 1959. The outcome was a disappointment for the Deputy Speaker Major Milner, Labour MP for South-East Leeds. He was offered (and accepted) a peerage instead. The resulting by-election was won by Denis Healey, who became an MP for the first time.

THE PARLIAMENTARY SESSION, 1951–2

The session lasted from 1 November 1951 until 31 October 1952. In addition to the usual recesses, parliament rose in early February on hearing of the king's death and did not resume normal business until

The formidable Bessie Braddock MP, seen here at a fashion show of 'Outsizes' with Gilbert Harding, the celebrated radio personality of the day.

19 February. Prime Minister's Question Time, which lasted fifteen minutes, was held on Tuesdays and Thursdays. The House of Commons normally rose at 10.30pm but in the period before Easter there were many late-night sessions. During one all-night sitting (26/7 March) Bessie Braddock, Labour representative for Liverpool Exchange, became the first woman MP to be suspended from the Commons after she had refused to obey the order to withdraw from the chamber. The guillotine was imposed on the Licensed Premises in New Towns Bill and the National Health Service Bill. The latter extended government powers to recover charges for services such as the provision of drugs and dental care. There were exemptions, however, which included expectant mothers and those under twenty-one.

HOME POLICY: THE LEGISLATIVE PROGRAMME, 1951–2

The first legislation to receive the royal assent was the Home Guard Act which established the Home Guard on a voluntary and limited basis in time of peace. Other laws passed during the course of this parliamentary session included improvements in family allowances, extended industrial injury benefits and increased Exchequer subsidies and rate fund contributions for houses built by local authorities. It also permitted local authorities to sell council houses.

In response to the housing crisis New Towns had been developed in the postwar years. The Conservative government continued to be involved in this venture by playing a more important part in encouraging and part-funding New Town development. But under its licensed premises legislation, it ended its right to manage the liquor trade in New Towns while retaining such responsibilities (which dated back to the First World War) elsewhere. Similarly settlement in the Commonwealth overseas was encouraged by providing assistance for suitable emigrants.

MANAGING THE ECONOMY

Primarily as a result of the continuing costs of recovering from the Second World War, but also because of British participation in the Korean War (1950–3), increased expenditure on armaments and rising imports, the Conservatives faced a serious economic situation on their return to power. This was leading to greater inflation at home and a general balance of payments crisis. For the last quarter of 1951 the deficit was the heaviest on record. This called for drastic action or another devaluation would be likely within six months.

On 7 November the Minister of Food, Gwilym Lloyd-George, announced cuts in the meat, butter and sugar rations. At the same time the Chancellor of the Exchequer outlined measures to reduce imports and cut the allowance for tourist travel abroad by half – to £50 a year. (In early 1952 the travel allowance was again halved.) On the same day the Chancellor increased the bank rate from 2 to 2.5 per cent. In January 1952 hire purchase term controls were introduced for cars and most other consumer durables. But the situation continued to deteriorate and an early budget was required.

The measures announced by the Chancellor on 11 March 1952 sought to reduce both consumer and government expenditure. Food subsidies were cut from £410 million to £250 million, the increase in the cost of food being only partly offset by tax concessions and increased allowances such as tax relief to help retired people and those living on small fixed incomes. Hire purchase sales were restricted further, the bank rate was raised to 4 per cent, an excess profits levy was introduced and the rearmament programme slowed down. Partly as a result of the action taken, the year ended with a balance of payments surplus of £300 million, despite a 10 per cent fall in the volume of exports.

The attempts to reduce government expenditure were at times very thorough, if irksome. In response to cuts in its budget, and in an attempt to reduce its telephone bill, the Natural History Museum stipulated that trunk (long-distance) calls were only to be made by those of Principal Scientific Officer grade and above. No private calls were to be made between 10.30 and 12.00. Thereafter such outside calls were permitted but 'with restraint'. Other economy measures implemented by the museum during the course of 1952 included closing at 5pm rather than 6pm between November and February and a freeze on recruitment. Both as a further saving and to overcome the consequences of possible power cuts, staff were also urged to refrain from using the building's lifts during peak periods.

FOREIGN POLICY

The policies of the new government did not represent any real change from the ideas pursued by Attlee and his Foreign Secretary Ernest Bevin. It sought a favourable outcome in three vital relationships – with the United States, the Commonwealth and the Communist world. There was only limited interest in (and no involvement with) the first moves towards European integration. The European Coal and Steel Community had been formed in April 1951 and the European Defence Community agreement was signed in May 1952. Britain participated in neither.

Good relations with the United States remained at the heart of British foreign policy and this was essentially true for 1952.

TELEPHONE CHARGES

Quarterly telephone rental for a single exclusive line for a private residence ranged from £1 10s to £2 and included, free, 3s 1½d worth of local calls (up to 15 miles). The cost of trunk calls varied with distance but did not exceed 3s 9d by day (for three minutes) and 1s 6d between 6pm and 10.30pm.
The minimum cost for an overseas call (limited to Europe) ranged from 6s (France) to 30s (Greece).

President Truman and Prime Minister Churchill leave the White House arm in arm.

Certainly there was a warm friendship between Churchill and President Truman in his last year of office. Both were anxious to say a personal goodbye to each other to mark that occasion. This contrasted with the (publicly known) clash of personalities between Anthony Eden and Dean Acheson, US Secretary of State at this time.

British participation, along with other Commonwealth members under UN control, in the Korean War, began in 1950 in the rival claims for sovereignty over a unified peninsula asserted by the Soviet-backed People's Democratic Republic in the north of Korea and the US-backed Republic of Korea in the south. Peace talks had begun at Kaesong on 8 July 1951 and were subsequently adjourned to the village of Panmunjom. An armistice agreement, maintaining a divided Korea, was not to be signed there until 27 July 1953. After a visit to America in January 1952 Churchill confirmed that Britain would join the US in any retaliation should the truce be broken. But there were bitter clashes in November during the armistice talks over the repatriation of prisoners.

Churchill also attached a lot of importance to the Commonwealth. But it was already apparent that such dominions as Australia and (to a lesser extent) New Zealand were no longer so prepared to follow Britain's approach to foreign affairs. Both continued to support British policy in the Middle East but had their own ideas for the Pacific region. The ANZUS Pact (September 1951) showed how far links between these two countries and the United States had come. Britain was excluded, not even being allowed observer status.

THE LABOUR PARTY

The Labour Party had over one million individual members in 1952 (its highest ever), and over six million if trade union and affiliated society membership were included. Although it had lost the 1951 general election, it won back the London County Council in 1952. Nevertheless, this was a difficult year for many in the party because of the growing strength of those known as the 'Bevanites'.

The Bevanites were members of a loose left-wing alliance of backbench MPs and activists who gathered around Aneurin ('Nye') Bevan following his resignation as Minister of Labour in 1951 in protest against the introduction of National Health Service charges to meet defence costs. This was a particularly important point of principle for him as he had been the Minister of Health responsible for setting up the health service. Harold Wilson, then President of the Board of

Aneurin Bevan, while still Minister of Health, presenting prizes and certificates at Hammersmith Hospital and Postgraduate School.

Trade (and a future Labour prime minister) and John Freeman (a junior minister) resigned with him. Supporters favoured reduced defence expenditure and a more socialist domestic policy. They first made their presence felt in March 1952 during a vote on the government's Defence Estimates. The official Labour line was to abstain but fifty-seven left-wing Labour backbenchers voted against.

Following his resignation Bevan wrote *In Place of Fear*. Published in April 1952, this work, while accepting the mixed economy, called for increased public ownership and greater industrial democracy. It also revealed Bevan's deep commitment to parliamentary democracy which he believed was in danger while economic power remained in private hands. The present situation, he argued, meant that parliament was 'the public mourner for private economic crimes'. The prevailing economic structure, he went on to say, threatened political participation as 'people have no use for a freedom which cheats them of redress'. Above all, under the present system the state had no income of its own. Consequently in the battle between society's need and personal greed the balance of power lay with the voter-taxpayer. This would normally be to the detriment of society's need. (Labour) governments, he continued, should find ways of raising money at source before it reached the public.

In Place of Fear was in great demand and translated into several languages. Not surprisingly, at the Labour Party Conference at Morecambe in October there were calls for the National Executive to draw up a list of key industries to be taken into public ownership by a future Labour government in order to secure the government's own source of revenue. This followed on from a resolution passed in the previous month by the Trades Union Congress at their annual conference which had called for further social ownership of (monopoly) industries and services.

Sir Stafford CRIPPS   *RIP 1952*

Born in 1889, Cripps was known as the 'Red Squire' in the 1930s because of his background, his extreme left-wing outlook and his advocacy of Popular Front politics. On readmission to the Labour Party in 1945 he was within two years to become Chancellor of the Exchequer and the personification of austerity, given his tall, gaunt look. From 1940 to 1942 he was British Ambassador to the Soviet Union and was in office thereafter. He led a Cabinet mission to India which prepared the way for its independence the following year. Declared medically unfit for the army in 1914, he had spent much of the First World War in France with the Red Cross. His health continued to be poor periodically thereafter, and he died in a Swiss clinic.

Hugh Gaitskell.

Above all, at this conference the Bevanites won six constituency places on the National Executive Committee. Bevan headed the voting and was joined by Harold Wilson, Dick Crossman and Barbara Castle. Herbert Morrison, Hugh Gaitskell (a future leader of the party), Manny Shinwell and Jim Callaghan (a future Labour prime minister) were among those defeated. Gaitskell accused one-sixth of the constituency delegates of being Communist or fellow-travellers. The Parliamentary Labour Party replied by voting to disband all unofficial party groupings. Two of the major trade unions used their block vote to support the leadership. Arthur Deakin of the Transport Workers reminded the delegates of the union's financial importance to the party while Sir William Lawther of the mineworkers, when heckled from the audience, shouted back 'Shut your gob!' In November Herbert Morrison defeated Bevan's challenge for the deputy leadership by 194 to 82 votes.

THE LIBERAL PARTY AND OTHERS

The 1951 general election represented one of the worst moments in the history of the party. Only around 2.5 per cent of voters had supported it. It had gained one seat but lost four and, with the sole exception of Jo Grimond, none of the six Liberal MPs was returned in the face of Conservative opposition. The party fared equally disastrously in municipal elections, with about 1.5 per cent of borough councillors in 1952.

There were no national party representatives from Wales or Scotland. But two nationalists were returned in Northern Ireland, as was a candidate from the Irish Labour Party. Mr Beattie won the normally Unionist seat of West Belfast by twenty-five votes, probably because a member of the Stormont Parliament was reported to have used the ancient Orange Order slogan 'To Hell with the Pope' during the campaign. Although repudiated by Unionists, such sentiments probably deterred any significant split in the Catholic vote. The remaining nine MPs from Ulster were all Unionists and as such were integrated into what was then the Conservative and Unionist Party.

The Last Farewell

THE MAN WHO WAS NOT EXPECTED TO BE KING

Albert Frederick Arthur George Saxe-Coburg was born on 14 December 1895 – thirty-four years to the day after the death of his great-grandfather, after whom (like other descendants) he was named. Prince Albert (or 'Bertie' as he was known in the family) was the second son of the future King George V and Queen Mary. Following a conventional private education predominantly under a Norfolk schoolmaster, he trained for the Royal Navy and saw action aboard HMS Collingwood (where he was known to all as Mr Johnson) during the Battle of Jutland (1916). In 1918 he joined the Royal Naval Air Service (which was subsequently to become part of the Royal Air Force) and was the first British prince to qualify as a pilot.

After a short period of study at Trinity College, Cambridge (the same college that Charles, Prince of Wales, was to attend), he began to undertake public duties with a particular interest in industrial matters, notably the Industrial Welfare Society. He became its president and often attended summer camps where boys from mills and factories mixed with those from public schools. A close and influential friendship developed with Louis Greig who was similarly minded, had also served in the RAF and with whom, among other things, Albert played tennis. Their skill enabled them to win the RAF Doubles Competition at Wimbledon in 1920.

Created Duke of York in the same year, he married Lady Elizabeth Bowes-Lyon, the youngest daughter of the Earl of Strathmore, in April 1923. They had two daughters – Elizabeth (born 1926) and Margaret (1930–2002). In 1927 the duke and duchess undertook a celebrated tour of Australia and New Zealand. After King George V's serious illness in 1928, the Duke of York, like his brothers, began to fulfil an increasing number of official engagements.

At the age of almost forty-one, the Duke of York became king on the abdication of his elder brother King Edward VIII in December 1936. He took the title King George VI. By temperament he was

King George VI.

King George VI and Queen
Elizabeth during their successful
visit to the USA in 1939.

somewhat highly strung – a characteristic that showed itself in a
stammer which diminished over time but could present difficulties
for all concerned during the course of some of the many speeches
which he was now required to deliver. He had not expected the
kingship, nor did he welcome the circumstances under which he
ascended the throne, being particularly fond of his elder brother.

The late 1930s was a period of increasing anxiety given the
continuing expansion and increasing military strength of Nazi
Germany. Like others, the king welcomed Neville Chamberlain's
efforts to save the peace and (despite divided opinion in the nation)
supported the Munich Agreement (1938) with Hitler which led to the
dismemberment of Czechoslovakia. Soon after the prime minister's
return from Germany, both men appeared together on the balcony of
Buckingham Palace to acknowledge the cheering crowds.

Shortly after Hitler completed his conquest of Czechoslovakia in
March 1939, the king and queen visited Canada and then crossed
into the United States at the invitation of President Roosevelt. This
was the first time a reigning British sovereign had visited that
country and the positive impact of the occasion did much to promote
good relations between these two nations.

The Second World War broke out a few months later in September
1939. While Windsor Castle was the king's war headquarters,
Buckingham Palace continued to be used. It was, contrary to Hitler's
orders, bombed in 1940. Their majesties' narrow escape, the damage

inflicted and the disruption experienced gave them some insight into what, as they toured the blitzed areas, so many of their subjects now faced. In doing this, the *New York Herald-Tribune* described them as 'Ministers of Morale'.

The demands of war on the king were considerable, especially as his health had never been strong. Furthermore, given his position, he was party to information which few others had access to during the dark days of the conflict and he felt acutely the personal consequences of war when encountering, through investitures, the relatives of those who had fallen in action. In recognition of the dangers faced and the courage displayed at home, George VI introduced a civilian equivalent to the Victoria Cross. Appropriately named the George Cross, its inscription was 'For Gallantry'.

In order to maintain close relations with his ministers, the king often dined at Downing Street. He continued to do this when Clement Attlee replaced Churchill as prime minister and enjoyed a good relationship with him. This was mutual: whenever Attlee spoke of the king's death, it was said, there were tears in his eyes and his voice. Although the king continued to carry out many engagements and to undertake overseas tours, he was often ill and underwent operations in March 1949 and September 1951. After the latter there was a day of National Thanksgiving on 2 December to mark his recovery but his health continued to cause concern.

THE LAST FAREWELL

The world tour which Princess Elizabeth and the Duke of Edinburgh began early in 1952 was originally to have been undertaken by the king himself. But his lung operation and convalescence meant that he was no longer able to fulfil the engagement. He confirmed the change in what was to be his last Christmas broadcast. For the first time, reflecting the king's continuing poor health, it had been pre-recorded in sections by the BBC.

The king returned to London from Sandringham in late January 1952 to see his doctors. They declared that they were 'very well satisfied' with their patient. This was a somewhat different prognosis, however, from that of the king's Private Secretary Alan Lascelles, who had warned Churchill earlier in the month, when he was in the United States visiting President Truman, that he considered the monarch's health to be in danger.

On 30 January the king and queen, together with their two daughters, the Duke of Edinburgh and Peter Townsend as King's Equerry in attendance, saw a performance of *South Pacific* at the Drury Lane Theatre, London. It was a double celebration – the king's

Princess Elizabeth and the Duke of Edinburgh leave Heathrow on 31 January 1952 for their trip to Kenya, seen off by the king on his first official engagement since his illness, accompanied by the queen and Princess Margaret.

continuing improvement and his daughter's imminent world tour. So it was that on a cold windy Thursday morning on the last day of January 1952 the king and queen were at London (Heathrow) Airport to wave goodbye to their daughter and son-in-law. This was to be the king's last appearance in public.

In addition to the king and queen, others witnessing the departure of their royal highnesses were Princess Margaret, the Duke and Duchess of Gloucester and Winston Churchill. The king, it was noted at the time, remained bareheaded until the flight, in a four-engined BOAC Argonaut airliner named *Atalanta*, took off at 12.11pm for Nairobi. This was the last time Princess Elizabeth saw her father alive.

The tour was to last until early July and, as well as Kenya, would take in Ceylon (now Sri Lanka), Australia, Tasmania and New

Zealand, returning home via Pitcairn Island and the Panama Canal. As with her parents' tour in 1927 it was not thought necessary for the princess to take the family.

DEATH OF A KING

On the following day the king and queen, with Princess Margaret, returned to Sandringham. Less than a week later, on Tuesday 5 February, with perfect weather and his health improving, the king decided to shoot hares. It was a successful day which ended with him sending congratulations to each of the keepers and planning the following day's sport. He retired to his room around 10.30 and to bed soon after midnight. But the coronary thrombosis he suffered that night meant that he never woke again.

It was at 7.30 in the morning on 6 February that his valet discovered the king was dead. The queen, in a neighbouring room, was the first to be informed. The king's Private Secretary used an agreed coded phrase ('Hyde Park Corner last night') to inform Edward Ford, the Assistant Private Secretary, of developments; he was to tell the prime minister in person. The king's mother, Queen Mary, was informed by one of her ladies-in-waiting.

Churchill was working in bed, surrounded by papers and a candle for his cigar. He took the news badly – King George had meant a lot to him. He called a Cabinet meeting for later that morning and informed all gathered accordingly. A second meeting was held in the afternoon when Churchill told his colleagues that the new queen was expected back in Britain the following day.

THE NEW QUEEN

Soon after Princess Elizabeth had arrived in Kenya she and the Duke of Edinburgh travelled to Forest Lodge, Sagana, over 100 miles from the capital Nairobi and a wedding present from the Government of Kenya. From there the couple went on to a hotel known as Treetops. Located in a remote site, the hotel's observation balcony enabled the couple to watch the wildlife around them. They were here when the king's heart attack occurred. It is said that the princess (although unconscious of her new status) was watching baboons when she acceded to the throne. It was four hours after the discovery that the king was dead (11.45am London time) that Prince Philip was able to inform his wife. This followed telephone calls between the prince's and princess's Private Secretaries. A telegram had been sent to Kenya with the same coded phrase as was used to alert Edward Ford but it was not received, possibly because it had been sent to Hyde

Earl Mountbatten addresses the Duke of Edinburgh as he and the new queen return after the death of the king, 7 February 1952.

Park Corner. Other members of the royal party were to learn of the king's death quite accidentally: one lady-in-waiting, aboard the *Gothic* in Mombasa in anticipation of the next stage of the visit, only learnt of it when she asked why people were removing decorations. Preparations were made for an immediate return to London.

At noon on Thursday 7 February, both at home and abroad, the death of the monarch was marked by a series of 56-gun salutes – each round representing a year of the late king's life. The salute at the Tower of London was fired by the 1st Regiment of The Honourable Artillery Company; in Hyde Park the King's Troop, Royal Horse Artillery, fired at one-minute intervals. The guns of ships of the Royal Navy and Service Stations throughout the world marked the occasion in a similar way.

The Queen and the Duke of Edinburgh flew back on the *Atalanta*. The queen changed into black just before landing. She had always taken mourning clothes with her since her father's operation a few months previously. She arrived at London airport at 4.30pm. Seeing the black limousines on the tarmac she is said to have exclaimed, 'Oh God, they've sent the hearses'. Among those who met the queen and duke were the prime minister, the leader of the opposition (Clement Attlee), Anthony Eden, the Duke of Gloucester (her uncle) and Lord and Lady Mountbatten. The new queen returned to Clarence House and spent thirty minutes with Queen Mary, who had already lived through five reigns and was now entering a sixth. She was staying at Marlborough House while the (present) Queen Mother and Princess Margaret were still at Sandringham.

In the evening Churchill made a broadcast to the nation. It was regarded as one of his finest. He described the impact of the king's death, the friendship which he had enjoyed with the late monarch, especially during the war years, and spoke of the king over the past few months having walked with death as if it were an acquaintance whom he did not fear. In the end death came as a friend. He then remarked that the 'Second Queen Elizabeth' was now ascending the throne, adding that she was almost the same age as her celebrated namesake when she had become queen. He concluded by observing that, as in his youth, he would once more utter the prayer and anthem GOD SAVE THE QUEEN.

'GOD SAVE THE QUEEN'

Churchill's utterance anticipated the outcome of the Accession Council which was held on Friday 8 February. The first meeting of the Privy Council was attended by almost 200 members. Hugh Dalton, a former Chancellor of the Exchequer, commented that the gathering included people 'one didn't remember were still alive', while Harold Wilson described it as the most moving ceremonial he could recall. The first public proclamation of Her Majesty Queen Elizabeth II was in Friary Court, St James's Palace, and followed the Privy Council meeting which had been held there.

The question of how the queen should be described in that proclamation had been discussed by the Cabinet on 7 February. George VI was the last King-Emperor. Titles and claims regarding overseas territories needed to be altered to reflect the changing realities of the British Empire and Commonwealth. The old wording included references to

Col Carkeet James, Resident Governor of the Tower of London, reads the queen's Proclamation at the Tower, 8 February 1952.

The Tudor crown (above), known as the king's crown, and St Edward's crown, known as the queen's.

Ireland which was now a republic outside the Commonwealth, while some of the territories concerned might no longer wish to be described as British Dominions.

George VI had only become 'Head of the Commonwealth' in 1951. In 1952 six self-governing nations in addition to the UK retained the British monarch as their head of state: Australia, Canada, Ceylon, New Zealand, Pakistan and South Africa. Changes featured in the nature of their proclamation which marked a move away from sovereignty over the Dominions to the queen enjoying a separate identity in each country.

Elizabeth was first proclaimed queen in Canada on 6 February itself. The proclamation in Ceylon, which had the oldest monarchy in the Commonwealth, was read in Sinhalese, Tamil and English. There was a twenty-one gun salute in South Africa, while the Republic of India proclaimed Queen Elizabeth II as Head of the Commonwealth. A twenty-one gun salute was fired in New Delhi to synchronise with the proclamation ceremonies in London.

The procedure in the UK began with the Friary Court declaration by the Garter King of Arms, Sir George Bellow, who announced that:

> The high and mighty Princess Elizabeth Alexandra Mary is now by the death of our late Sovereign of happy memory become Queen Elizabeth II, by the Grace of God Queen of this realm and her other realms and territories, head of the Commonwealth, Defender of the Faith.

The Lancaster Herald read the proclamation a second time at Trafalgar Square; the Norroy and Ulster King of Arms read it a third time at Temple Bar and the final rendering in the centre of the capital was by the Clarenceux King of Arms at the Royal Exchange.

The accession was proclaimed throughout the rest of the UK, often becoming a civic event in its own right. In Windsor the proclamation was read three times and on each occasion was accompanied by a guard of honour provided by the Life Guards together with a fanfare by trumpeters of the Royal Horse Guards. In Cardiff it was accompanied by a detachment of the Welch Regiment and witnessed by fifteen thousand children; in Caernarvon it was read in English and Welsh. In Lancashire, the County Palatine, the toast was 'The Queen, Duke of Lancaster'. In York the announcement was made four times. The first of these was marked by the Lord Mayor drinking the new queen's health from a seventeenth-century gold loving cup which he drained in one go. In Edinburgh there was a twenty-one gun salute with the castle proclamation read by the Albany Herald Sir Francis Grant. Born in 1864, Sir Francis had also proclaimed every sovereign since Edward VII (1901). Ely was probably the last place in the UK to announce the accession. This took place on 15 March and followed the sending of a petition, signed by nearly sixty prominent citizens of the area, to Ely Urban Council expressing annoyance that the occasion had not been marked by the city.

PAYING LAST RESPECTS: SANDRINGHAM

The king's coffin lay in the Church of St Mary Magdalene at Sandringham on 9 and 10 February. It rested on trestles before the altar and was draped with the royal standard. It had just three wreaths on it. One was of white orchids, lilies and carnations, from the Queen Mother; another was from Princess Margaret. At the head was the third wreath – of white lilies, tulips, hyacinths, Christmas roses and lilies of the valley, accompanied by a card signed 'Lilibet and Philip'.

The coffin was under the continuous watch of local people, including estate workers, gamekeepers and foresters. On 9 February workers and tenants had the opportunity to pay their last respects. The following day a brief private service was held in the presence of Queen Elizabeth, the Queen Mother and other members of the royal family.

THE JOURNEY TO WESTMINSTER HALL, LONDON

On 11 February the King's Company, 1st Battalion the Grenadier Guards, each member of which was at least 6ft 3in tall, took the coffin from the church to the waiting gun carriage. The Scottish lament 'The Flowers of the Forest' was played on the pipes as the coffin was escorted to Wolferton station for the journey to King's Cross, where it arrived at 2.45pm. The coffin was draped with the royal standard and the imperial state crown was placed on its centre. The station had been prepared, with the supporting pillars draped in black and purple cloth and adorned with laurel wreaths. No trains moved in or out of the station while the king's body was there. All signals were at stop.

On arrival, the coffin was transferred from the hearse coach to the waiting gun carriage. There was a cold drizzle as it and the accompanying cortège proceeded to Westminster Hall. The gun carriage was drawn by the King's Troop, Royal Horse Artillery, and was again flanked by Grenadier Guards. The imperial state crown was placed on the coffin along with a single wreath from the Queen Mother. The Dukes of Edinburgh and Gloucester (the late king's brother) walked behind in civilian clothes.

The route passed near London University and students from Britain, the Empire and Commonwealth countries gathered to watch

The four royal dukes walk behind the carriage conveying the Queen, the Queen Mother, Princess Margaret and the Princess Royal, as the king's funeral procession skirts the walls of Windsor Castle.

the procession. In Kingsway, Holborn, many of the shops had removed their goods and their windows displayed single draped portraits of the king accompanied by vases of white lilac, snowdrops or lilies. Thousands of silent people lined the route, mostly office workers and shop assistants. The arrival was watched by three mourning queens – mother, widow and daughter. Princess Margaret and the Duchess of Kent were also there. This event was recorded by photographers, an action seen by some as a 'new low' in the behaviour of the press.

PAYING LAST RESPECTS: WESTMINSTER HALL

The funeral was held on Friday 15 February. Until then George VI lay in state at Westminster Hall. The coffin rested on a purple catafalque and was draped in the royal standard. On top were the imperial crown, sceptre, orb and the wreath from the Queen Mother. Candles set in tall gold candlesticks (borrowed from the Tomb of the Unknown Warrior) burned continuously at the four corners, the head and the foot of the catafalque.

Throughout the period in Westminster Hall, four officers of Household Troops stood at each corner of the upper dais. At the same corners, but below the dais, were four members of the Yeomen

The body of King George VI lies in state in Westminster Hall, 11 February 1952.

Queen Mary and the Duke of Windsor leave Westminster Hall after paying their last respects to the king.

of the Guard. At the head of the catafalque were members of the King's Gentlemen at Arms. The guards were relieved every twenty minutes, reliefs replacing the officers on duty in silence.

On Tuesday 12 February the public were admitted from 8am. Despite the cold, rain, sleet and snow for much of the next few days, thousands of people were determined to say farewell. Originally the doors of Westminster Hall were to have closed at 10pm. But such were the queues that the hours of opening needed to be extended. On the first day it was initially agreed that the doors might stay open until 11pm. But as this would have disappointed so many, it was decided to close the queue instead – which at 11pm was 200 yards south of Lambeth Bridge. Finally the doors closed on the first day at 1.45am. Over 76,000 people had passed through.

On the Wednesday the queue could be joined until midnight, with the doors closing at 3.20am. Some 108,000 people visited that day, including Queen Mary, the Duke of Windsor (another of the late king's brothers) and Mary, the Princess Royal (his sister). On the Thursday the doors were again opened to enable people to file past and did not close again until 6am the following day, the day of the funeral itself.

The queen and Princess Margaret visited Westminster Hall on the eve of the funeral, staying for ten minutes. The Queen Mother came just before midnight and stayed some twenty minutes. Others who paid their respects during these days included Dr Fisher, the Archbishop of Canterbury, Cardinal Griffin, the Archbishop of

Westminster, General Eisenhower, President Auriol of France and Dr Adenauer of the Federal Republic of Germany.

At its greatest, the queue stretched from Westminster Hall over Lambeth Bridge, down the Albert Embankment past St Thomas's Hospital to Westminster Bridge and doubled back round Lambeth Palace. This meant that at times the queue was over 4 miles long. Members of the British Red Cross were stationed nearby and in Westminster Hall to aid any in need of their assistance. Only in the last few hours (2.30am to 6am) on 15 February was there immediate entry. In all some 305,806 people came to Westminster Hall as a token of respect for the king and the person he was.

THE FUNERAL PROCESSION, LONDON AND WINDSOR

On the morning of Friday 15 February, the king's coffin was transferred from Westminster Hall by a bearer party of the Brigade of Guards and placed on a gun carriage drawn by naval ratings. This tradition had arisen from a spontaneous response to the last minute tangled harnesses which had prevented the use of the horses which were to have drawn the gun carriage at Queen Victoria's funeral in February 1901.

The procession from Westminster to Paddington began at 9.30. It was led by the Earl Marshal, the Duke of Norfolk, the premier duke of England. There were seven reigning sovereigns, three Heads of State and three Crown Princes in the cortège. The procession also included the heads of foreign delegations led by Mr Zaroubin, the Soviet Ambassador; High Commissioners representing Common-wealth countries and Dean Acheson, the United States Secretary of State. Three field marshals, Viscount Montgomery, Lord Ironside and Viscount Alanbrooke, General de Gaulle (at the time out of office) and General Eisenhower were also there. In the procession beside the gun carriage were the late king's equerries, including Viscount Althorp and Group Captain Peter Townsend.

In the pale winter sunshine, the cortège travelled up Whitehall, along the Mall and Piccadilly through Hyde Park to Paddington to the strains of the funeral airs of Handel and Chopin. Thousands, many dressed in black, lined the route. Some had waited in the streets all night to get a good view, but others just caught a glimpse as the procession passed by – though sometimes with the aid of a periscope. The St John Ambulance Brigade and the Red Cross were again on hand and treated 450 casualties along the route from White-hall to Paddington. Ten were taken to hospital with broken arms.

At Paddington the coffin was transferred to a waiting train whose engine (no. 4082 *Windsor Castle*) had a replica of the imperial state

The king's funeral procession leaves Horse Guards Parade en route to Paddington station, 15 February 1952.

crown on its front and the royal coat of arms on its side. At Windsor the coffin was escorted from the station through to the Sovereign's Entrance, Windsor Castle, and on to St George's Chapel.

THE FUNERAL SERVICE

The funeral service began at 2pm. At exactly that moment two minutes' silence was held throughout the kingdom: at Lloyds, for example, the Lutine Bell was rung to call a halt to business while at the Natural History Museum it was marked in the Central ('Dinosaur') Hall where staff as well as public could gather. Services were held throughout the country at or around that time. A form of the funeral service was also prepared by the (then) National Institute for the Blind for some seventy blind clergy and organists in the country. There were also services overseas: President and Mrs Truman attended one at Washington Cathedral.

The silence was followed by the firing of maroons. The twenty-minute service was led by the Dean of Windsor (Bishop Hamilton). Other ecclesiastics in the procession included the Archbishops of Canterbury and York and the Moderators of the Church of Scotland and the Free Church Federal Council. The prime minister was in the congregation dressed as Warden of the Cinq Ports. Following medical advice, Queen Mary did not attend the funeral but watched

Princess Margaret and the Queen Mother veiled in black as they are driven to Westminster Hall to meet the coffin of the late king, 11 February 1952.

the cortège from her home, Marlborough House, and followed the broadcast. Prince Charles, now Duke of Cornwall following his grandfather's death, was at Sandringham.

The Committal, the most poignant moment of the service, involved the Lord Chamberlain as well as the queen. The former held his stick of office at arm's length, broke it in two and set both halves on the coffin. The colour of the King's Company, Grenadier Guards, was laid on the coffin by the queen. She was handed a silver bowl containing red earth and she sprinkled the contents on to the coffin as it sank into the vault beneath. The service ended with the roll call of the late king's titles, prayers for the new monarch and a rendering of *God Save the Queen*. After the coffin had been lowered into the vault it was conveyed to its resting place in the royal tomb-house, which lies beneath the Albert Memorial Chapel. The tomb-house, built by George III, was designed to hold eighty-one bodies.

The congregation dispersed. Some, but not the Duke of Windsor, were invited back to the funeral dinner at Buckingham Palace. The duke stayed in Britain for only a few days. He had been in New York when the news of his brother's death broke and came to the funeral alone. He had meetings with his mother and with the Queen Mother whom he referred to as 'Cookie' in his letters to Wallis, Duchess of Windsor. There was no real sense of any reconciliation between the duke and the royal family. He left London a disappointed and poorer man – a major consequence of his brother's death was that he would no longer receive the £10,000 annual allowance which had been made by the late king.

AFTERMATH

For a few days after the funeral there was a public display at Windsor Castle of the thousands of wreaths which had been sent as a mark of respect. These ranged from a floral George Cross from the British government to some snowdrops from a group of children living in Bermondsey, London. The government's wreath, in white lilac and white lilies, read 'For Valour' – the inscription on the Victoria Cross – in Churchill's own handwriting.

The castle gates opened at 9am to a 3 mile queue. At 4pm, an hour before the gates were due to close, the police sealed it off – much to the anger of many of those who had waited so long. It was estimated that there were 10,000 people inside the gates at that time forming a line almost 2 miles long. On the following day, amidst pouring rain, some 150,000 entered the castle grounds. In order to ensure that all might see the tributes, floodlighting was installed to extend the opening hours.

THE KING'S DEATH AND FUNERAL – WIDER IMPACT

As on other such occasions, many people could and still can recall what they were doing when they learned of the king's death. Many gathered outside 10 Downing Street on 6 February itself, while others went to Westminster Palace Yard. A newspaper placard proclaiming the king's death fell over outside the entrance to an underground station. It was noticed that people walked around it. A special issue of the *London Gazette* was on sale. It consisted of a single sheet with a black border recording the king's death.

The bell of St Paul's Cathedral tolled for two hours; so did the Lutine Bell at Lloyds when they heard the news and the under-writing room closed at noon. Some shops in the West End changed their bright window displays to reflect the more sombre mood of their customers. While hotels and restaurants remained open, many music, dancing and other entertainments were cancelled that day and for longer.

Indeed, the event had a very real impact on many aspects of life during the ten days between the king's death and his funeral, both at home and abroad. The United States' House of Representatives carried unanimously a resolution of sympathy and adjourned immediately on learning of the news, as did the parliament in India. The prime minister of the Irish Republic, Eamon de Valera, on 13 February asked the Dail to extend its sympathy to the royal family, parliament and people of Great Britain. The Irish Senate passed a similar motion.

Eamon de Valera.

Unlike the accession of Queen Victoria (1837), that of Queen Elizabeth II did not necessitate a general election. His Majesty might be dead, but His (or Her) Majesty's Government was unaffected. Even so, on the morning of 6 February the sittings of both Houses of Parliament were cancelled. On the same day members began to take the oath of allegiance to Queen Elizabeth II. Messages of condolence to the queen and Queen Mother were passed. Both Houses resumed normal business on Tuesday 19 February.

While politics at Westminster were suspended, those seeking to be elected continued to campaign, albeit less intensely. There were two by-elections on the day of the king's death (at Bournemouth East and Southport) and one the following day at Leeds South-East, which Denis Healey was contesting. The loudspeakers there were silenced and plans for a final burst of campaigning were abandoned. The turn-out was lower but Healey was victorious. Another winner earlier in his campaign was chosen by Mr Healey himself in a young socialists' speaking contest – Betty Boothroyd, a future MP and Speaker of the House of Commons.

On 12 February the queen sent a message to all civil servants expressing 'warm thanks' for carrying out their duties during her father's reign and stated that their loyalty and steadfastness would be her 'enduring support'. The Natural History Museum informed its staff of the king's demise on the day, adding that following a decision taken in 1936 the Trustees had decided not to close the museum on the death of the sovereign. It would also be open on the day of the funeral. Subsequently it notified them that black-edged notepaper was not generally to be used unless in communicating with her majesty's representatives overseas or representatives of foreign governments. In the interests of economy, stationery marked On His Majesty's Service was to be used until stocks were exhausted.

The armed services were also affected. Military bands were not to play nor were bugles to be used at the hoisting of the colours. All courts of the Central Criminal Court ('the Old Bailey') adjourned and Scotland Yard instructed all ranks from inspector upwards in the Metropolitan Police to wear black crepe armbands.

A reunion dinner of the survivors of the destroyer HMS *Kelly* had been arranged at the (then) Over-Seas League by its president (and the ship's captain) Lord Mountbatten. The BBC had arranged to feature some of the survivors in its programme *In Town Tonight* before the dinner took place and the reunion was to have been filmed by a newsreel company. All this was postponed because of national mourning. Similarly the Horse and Hounds Ball was postponed until 28 March. The Ruskin Society, however, met as planned to mark the

An open day was held at the Stock Exchange on 19 April 1952, hence the visitors.

critic's birthday but paid tribute to the king's memory during its proceedings.

On the day of the funeral the Stock Exchange was closed, as were many shops. The Bond Street Association (retailers) recommended that, other than food shops, its members should close all day. The London Co-operative Society's 1,200 shops and departments were closed from 1 to 3 in the afternoon while chemists were shut from 10am until 4pm. Schools and factories were encouraged to continue to operate. Many schools, however, closed, especially in Wales, and others held short services. Work stopped in shops and factories to observe the two minutes' silence. Miners for instance observed it throughout the coalfields, with trams and cages being halted. Merseyside dockers in the holds of ships stopped work to 'thank God for this good life devotedly spent in our service'.

THE MEDIA

The three BBC radio stations were temporarily merged and adopted a sombre, limited and rather repetitive schedule. While *On Your Farm* was retained, *Mrs Dale's Diary* and *Music While You Work* were not. At a memorial service for the king held on 14 February, the Roman Catholic Bishop of Leeds John Heenan (a future Cardinal Archbishop of Westminster) criticised the BBC for having 'wrapped the nation in organised gloom for more than a week. The death of a constitutional monarch need not paralyse the legitimate relaxation of the whole nation for so long.' He also referred to the 'melodrama of prolonged silences on the day of [the king's] death and the subsequent mirthless programmes on offer without alternatives'.

Radio (and television) coverage on matters relating to the death and funeral were indeed quite extensive. Schedules for both were affected, albeit *Andy Pandy* continued to be shown on television. The Royal Horse Artillery salute of 7 February was televised live and Churchill's speech to the nation that evening was broadcast on both radio and television (sound only). There was television coverage of the cortège in Westminster Hall and of part of the route to Paddington. But although some scenes from Windsor Castle were included, the funeral service was in sound only. As only about one in six households had a television, neighbours were in many cases invited in by those lucky enough to possess one. One elderly couple who accepted such an offer both died as they watched the event unfold.

The BBC Northern Regional Controller received a reprimand for claiming subsequently in the *Radio Times* that the Corporation's handling of the funeral was likely to have been well received by the royal family. The outlook from the palace was that the royal family did not have a view on broadcasting, nor should one be attributed to them. The Director General Sir William Haley ordered that the journal should never again carry articles on this subject.

The funeral was broadcast live to certain countries and recorded for subsequent transmission elsewhere at a more convenient time. The major US broadcasting organisations had commentators along the route. The BBC gave advance notice of its broadcasting plans to Eastern Europe in the hope that the Russian and Polish authorities would not jam its coverage; but about half the transmitters were jammed.

The government recognised that the demand for newspapers and periodicals would increase at this time, and that many might wish to carry features and prepare special issues to mark the events of these days together with the life of the late king and his successor. But given the economic difficulties, access to paper was under Strict government control. On 8 February the Newsprint Rationing Committee announced that extra supplies would be made available. These could be used for increased circulation or additional pages subject only to the statutory regulations on maximum sizes contained in the Control of Paper (Newspapers) (Economy) Order 1949.

Other entertainment, leisure and sporting activities were also affected. The Lord Chamberlain directed that those theatres licensed by him should close on 6 February and remain so until 6pm on the day of the funeral. Private theatres tended to follow the example of public ones. The Cinematograph Exhibitors' Association advised its members to do the same. Institutions and organisations were to mark the occasion either immediately or later in the year – there was, for instance, no Royal Academy dinner in 1952 (although the opportunity to save money was also welcomed as investments worth £10,000 had to be sold that year to reduce their overdraft).

The impact on sport was considerable. The Scottish Rugby Union advised that matches should be cancelled and all those due to be played in Wales actually were. The England v. Ireland rugby union match planned for 9 February at Twickenham was postponed. The All-England Women's Hockey Association decided that no matches should be played until after the funeral, while the Squash Racquets Association postponed its England v. Ireland match. No professional boxing tournaments under the British Board of Boxing Control took place on 6 February. There were no National Hunt horse-race meetings until after the funeral, but greyhound racing was only cancelled on 6 February itself.

Football Association cup ties scheduled to be played on the night of 6 February took place but were preceded by both players and

The British team at the opening ceremony of the VIth Winter Olympics, wearing black armbands to acknowledge the king's recent death, 15 February 1952.

spectators paying tribute to the king. Indeed, football matches generally continued to be played up to 14 February unless both teams agreed not to. Where games went ahead, the Association recommended that 'Abide with Me' be played by bands or loudspeaker. This was to be followed by one minute's silence and then the National Anthem. The players were to wear black armbands. Details of what was to happen were to be included in the football programme and the local press informed. The winter Olympic Games opened officially on 15 February and the flags of all competing nations were dipped in homage to the late king.

THE CHURCHES AND COURT MOURNING

The death and funeral of the king were acknowledged by the various Christian churches and by other faiths. Prayers for the late king were recited in all synagogues on Saturday 9 February while a special service was held in the West End synagogue on the day of the funeral. Also on that day there was a 3pm service at St Margaret's, the parish church for the Houses of Parliament, which was open to members of both Houses, representative bodies and the public (the latter seated separately in the nave). The Salvation Army held a service in the Festival Hall at the same time.

Over this period there were also services at both the Russian Orthodox Church in Buckingham Palace Road and the Greek

Cardinal Griffin, Archbishop of Westminster.

Orthodox Cathedral in Moscow Road, London. Cardinal Griffin, the Archbishop of Westminster, officiated at a benediction in his cathedral on 10 February. Special services were also held by Methodists and the Chancellor of the Exchequer preached a sermon on the late king in his village church. The BBC held its own memorial service on the evening of Sunday 10 February. It was preceded by an address by Dr Fisher, the Archbishop of Canterbury.

It was announced on 9 February that the Court would be in mourning until 31 May. At less than four months it was shorter than that for earlier twentieth-century monarchs. It had been six months each of mourning and half-mourning for Edward VII (1910) and six months and three months respectively for George V (1936). Once the mourning was over, the new Elizabethan era, as these days were heralded, could truly begin.

THE NEW ELIZABETHANS

In its issue of 19 April 1952, *Picture Post* carried a feature on those whom it termed New Elizabethans. These were people who, although they might already have made their mark, would become leading figures in their field during the reign which had just begun. Among those identified were:

politician	R.A. Butler; Nye Bevan
composer	Benjamin Britten; William Walton
poet	C. Day Lewis
novelist	Graham Greene
dramatist	Christopher Fry
painter	Graham Sutherland
cartoonist	(Carl) Giles
art historian	Kenneth Clark
sculptor	Henry Moore
philosopher	A.J. Ayer
racing driver	Stirling Moss
ballerina	Margot Fonteyn
film director	Carol Reed
actress	Celia Johnson
actor	Alec Clunes; Alec Guinness; Glynis Johns

FOUR

Life of a Queen

GIRLHOOD

Elizabeth Alexandra Mary was born at 2.40am on 21 April 1926 at 17 Bruton Street, London, the home of her maternal grandparents. She was the first daughter of the Duke and Duchess of York and the birth was attended by the then Home Secretary Joynson-Hicks. Although Elizabeth was third in line to the throne at birth, her succession was not looked on at that time as more than a remote possibility.

After a brief stay in her father's London home at 145 Piccadilly, she spent most of her early life at the Royal Lodge at Windsor. She was a particular favourite of her grandfather George V, who, like other members of the family, called her 'Lilibet', a name she had devised herself at the age of two. There were only a few public appearances in the first ten years of her life – she took part in the Silver Jubilee procession (1935) and in the king's funeral the following year. Her 'Uncle David' ascended the throne as Edward VIII but his abdication before the year was out meant her position as the future monarch was assured. Her general education was in the hands of an experienced governess, Miss Marion Crawford, known to the public as 'Crawfie'.

The princess, along with her sister Margaret, went to Scotland at the beginning of the Second World War for fear of air raids on London. Later they left to live at Windsor. It was from there that Elizabeth made her first broadcast, aged fourteen, in 1940. It was a short talk addressed primarily to British children who were separated from their families. At sixteen, wearing her Girl Guide uniform, she registered for National Service and was subsequently allowed by her father to join the Mechanical Transport Training Centre at Aldershot where she learnt to drive and service army vehicles.

The future queen's earliest public engagements without her parents took place in May 1944. She spoke publicly for the first time at the annual meeting of the Queen Elizabeth Hospital for

Jubilee day in 1935 saw the Duke and Duchess of York, accompanied by their children, at St Paul's Cathedral to mark the jubilee of King George V.

children in Hackney and soon afterwards was installed as President of the National Society for the Prevention of Cruelty to Children. The following year she featured prominently (as well as not so prominently) in celebrations to mark the end of the war in Europe. On 8 May itself the two sisters, with a small escort, walked through the crowded streets of central London unrecognised, did the hokey-cokey and the Lambeth Walk, and ended up at the palace gates to join in the excited shouts of 'We want the King'.

Princess Elizabeth's first tour was to South Africa where she spent her twenty-first birthday. She marked the occasion with a broadcast to the British Empire in which she promised to dedicate her life to the service of the British Commonwealth. The speech, written by Sir Alan Lascelles, George VI's Private Secretary, was a great success and initiated a genuine love for those countries.

Later in 1947 the princess took part in her first Trooping of the Colour and on 9 July her engagement to Lieutenant Philip Mountbatten RN was announced. Formerly Prince Philip of Greece, he was a distant relation of his future wife through Queen Victoria and the princess had known him since she was a girl. They were married in Westminster Abbey four months later. On the morning of the wedding Prince Philip became the Duke of Edinburgh and less than a year later a father. During 1949 the young family moved to Clarence House (near St James's Palace) and it was here that Princess Anne was born in August 1950.

At the start of October 1951 the Duke and Duchess of Edinburgh were to sail to Canada to begin a tour there which would also take in Washington. But the serious nature of the king's operation on 23 September delayed their start. It was then suggested that in order to keep to the tour's schedule they should fly. The prime minister, Clement Attlee, was agreeable but Churchill had his doubts about the heir to the throne flying across the Atlantic. When the Duke of Edinburgh learnt of this he pointed out that Churchill had flown to North America during the Second World War and that he had been of greater significance to the nation then than they were now. The couple eventually flew to Canada on 7 October, but remained conscious of the king's serious state of health. Indeed, throughout

Princess Elizabeth and the Duke of Edinburgh meet a Mountie as they board the train to Quebec during their Canadian tour, 1951.

the visit the princess's Private Secretary, Major Martin Charteris, kept papers under his bed about the holding of an Accession Council. The tour was demanding but, despite these circumstances, it was something of a success. The Canadians declared 'We send you back a new princess'. The *Washington Evening Star* carried the remark made by President Truman: 'When I was a little boy, I read about a fairy princess, and there she is.' Her next return from an overseas visit was to be premature, in mourning and as queen.

ELIZABETH . . . WHO?

The queen's decision to use her first name was welcome, but its number and the title of the Royal House were to cause some resentment and frustration. While she was the second Queen of England to bear that name, Elizabeth I had not been Queen of Scotland which was then an independent nation. Therefore, it was argued, the new queen's correct title north of the border was Queen Elizabeth I. On 11 February the Scottish Covenant Association issued a solemn protest over her majesty's title in the territory. Such proclamations declaring her the second Elizabeth over Scotland denied 'the facts of history [and] have flouted the sentiments of Her Majesty's loyal Scottish people'. It went on to say that her advisers appeared to treat them as 'a people subjugated by and made subordinate to the people of England'. In some Scottish towns, after representations by the Scottish Covenant movement, the Provosts omitted from the proclamation any reference to the word 'Second'. In Alva, near Stirling, the prayers identified Elizabeth as the 'I of Scotland and II of England'.

The other issue concerned what the royal family and its descendants should be called. Taking Queen Victoria's husband's house name (Saxe-Coburg-Gotha) as precedent, the then Lord Chancellor had said at the time of the princess's marriage in 1947 that any children would bear Philip's name, Mountbatten. But almost as soon as the reign began, there were difficulties within the family over whether the House of Windsor, Edinburgh or Mountbatten now held the throne. The queen, like her three predecessors, was a Windsor (as Saxe-Coburg-Gotha had been renamed in 1917) while Edinburgh was a recent royal creation favoured by Philip himself. Mountbatten was an anglicised version of the German Battenberg, also dating from the First World War and much favoured by 'Uncle Dickie' (Earl Mountbatten), who was heard to boast at a house party held at his home, Broadlands in Hampshire, that the House of Mountbatten now reigned.

Such a comment annoyed and worried the queen's grandmother, Queen Mary, who in turn brought this claim to the prime minister's

The Duke of Edinburgh at Helsinki for the Olympic Games, July 1952.

attention. Churchill distrusted Mountbatten, seeing him both as a rival and as a failure in India where he had been the last viceroy (1947). Despite a memorandum from the Duke of Edinburgh himself, the Cabinet supported Churchill in seeking to retain the Windsor nomenclature and he reported back on 20 February that the queen had agreed. On 10 April it was reported officially that at a recent meeting of the Privy Council she announced that she wished her family and descendants to be known as Windsor. Prince Philip was reported to be furious, describing himself as being nothing 'but a bloody amoeba'.

HER FIRST DAYS AS QUEEN

The Court was in mourning until 31 May and, while she was kept busy, the duties which the queen fulfilled in the intervening period rarely involved crowds. The first document she had signed as queen related to an army buggery case. Her first public engagement as queen was on 10 April when she was accompanied by the Duke of Edinburgh to distribute Maundy Money in Westminster Abbey. Although it was an ancient ceremony, the monarch's active participation in it had lapsed from the late seventeenth century until the time of the queen's grandfather George V, who had re-established this custom just twenty years earlier in 1932.

A crowd of 5,000 witnessed the event. The queen distributed the coins to twenty-six men and twenty-six women, one pair for each year of her life. There were four specially minted silver pieces. In addition to the Maundy Money, each recipient was also given

The queen attends the Maundy service, her first public engagement since her accession, 10 April 1952.

ordinary coins. This was another long-standing tradition, the money having replaced a gift of clothes. Similarly long abandoned was the washing of the people's feet, a conscious echo of what Christ did for His disciples at the Last Supper, although the Lord High Almoner and his assistants, who were responsible for charitable acts by the monarch, still carried white towels with them at the service as a relic of this deed. The queen also had with her the traditional posy of herbs and spring flowers chosen and prepared by her herbalist. This also recalled a remote time when the posy was designed to ward off plague.

Easter was spent at Windsor. The queen's first ceremonial parade occurred there on her birthday and involved her last inspection of the Grenadier Guards as Colonel of the Regiment. She had held that position since she was sixteen. As queen she held the colonelcy-in-chief of all the Guards regiments. The ceremony took place in the rain and was watched by Prince Charles, Princess Anne, Princess Margaret and the Queen Mother. A few days later there was a gathering of Queen's Scouts at the castle. The queen took the salute in the presence of the Chief Scout Lord Rowallan.

Towards the end of April the queen attended the Badminton Horse Trials as a guest of the Duke of Beaufort and watched the British Olympic team in action. She also presented a bronze statuette of Foxhunter to Lieutenant-Colonel Harry Llewellyn. This was awarded to him by the British Show Jumping Association in recognition of him being awarded the title of 'Leading Rider in Europe' for the third year running – the first time any rider had been so honoured. While in the area the queen visited the Severn Wildfowl Trust at Slimbridge, Gloucestershire, which had been founded by Peter Scott (son of Captain Scott the explorer) in 1946. Here she saw the five trumpeter swans which had been presented to her during her recent Canadian tour.

THE MOVE TO BUCKINGHAM PALACE

Both Queen Elizabeth and the Duke of Edinburgh were reluctant to leave their home, Clarence House, and had hoped to use Buckingham Palace solely for work and receptions. But Churchill was opposed to such an approach and the monarch moved accordingly. The Queen Mother also continued in residence there.

Concurrent with the move and settling in to their new home there was growing anxiety over the potential conflict between the responsibilities of being a mother and a monarch. The National Federation of Women's Institutes highlighted this dilemma in the first resolution carried at the Federation's AGM held in July 1952. It read: 'That this meeting, remembering that our young Queen has duties as a wife and mother, urges the nation as a whole not to overwork Her Majesty.' The medical journal *The Lancet* also supported this outlook – that the queen should put her family first and that her advisers should limit her official presence to important occasions.

PREPARATIONS FOR THE CORONATION

The greatest pending occasion was the coronation. Its timing was first discussed in Cabinet on 11 February – even before the late king's funeral. Holding it in 1952 was ruled out primarily because it would detract from the government's focus on the economy. There might also be political advantage in delaying it until the summer of 1953. The government hoped that enthusiasm for the event would benefit the Conservatives in the next general election which was likely to be held (and indeed was) in 1955. Furthermore Churchill, almost seventy-seven when becoming prime minister again, had originally hinted at resigning after about a year in office (which would take him to October 1952). But now he was less eager to go. He delighted in both the premiership and his relationship with the new monarch, perhaps seeing similarities with his predecessor Lord Melbourne and the young Queen Victoria. Certainly he relished and tended to prolong his weekly audiences with the queen, especially if, as was often the case, the subject matter extended beyond politics to mutual interests such as horse racing and polo.

Churchill's doctor noted that the prime minister was determined to see the coronation before retiring but now (perhaps understandably) at the same time he sought to delay the ceremony for as long as possible. Other countries where Queen Elizabeth reigned, however, notably Australia and New Zealand, hoped that she would visit them soon – but after she had been crowned.

Late May 1953 was a distinct possibility at one time for the coronation but this presented various problems, including the timing of the Whitsun Bank Holiday which would fall on the last Monday of that month. The Cabinet opposed holding the coronation in the same week because of the ensuing lost productivity. Consequently the following Tuesday (2 June) was chosen. People who needed to travel to London could therefore do so on the Monday which would be both easier and, not being a Sunday, less controversial . . . and Wednesday 3 June was Derby Day.

The coronation date was formally announced on 28 April and the coronation proclamation was issued at the four traditional sites in London (St James's Palace, Charing Cross, Temple Bar and the Royal

Exchange) in early June. A Coronation Committee was created and chaired by the Duke of Edinburgh. It had thirty-six members including representatives from the UK, Canada, Australia, New Zealand, Pakistan and Ceylon. Members included the Archbishop of Canterbury (Dr Fisher), Winston Churchill, Clement Attlee, Lord Woolton and Earl Jowitt.

The committee's remit was quite wide and various sub-committees were established, including one under the 16th Duke of Norfolk who, as hereditary Earl Marshal, was to play a key role in the preparations. But at least one crucial element in the ceremony was back in place. On Christmas morning 1950 the Stone of Scone had been removed from Westminster Abbey, its traditional resting place at that time, by three Scottish students. It was recovered in April 1951 in Scotland. Shortly afterwards it was returned to (but hidden in) the Abbey. On 26 February 1952 the stone was replaced under the Coronation Chair. It was padlocked to the chair by means of an inch-thick chain threaded through the iron loops. There were also warning devices, some of them secret, in case anyone attempted to tamper with it again.

The Stone of Scone.

The year-long lead-up to the coronation was deliberate as both the administrative and commercial preparations (notably the manufacture of souvenirs and street decorations) were extensive. Already in March 1952 a Covent Garden company had begun restoring robes which would be hired by peers and peeresses for the occasion. These had been acquired from previous owners and were kept in waterproof boxes in strong-rooms under neighbouring streets.

There was also the issue of television coverage of the event. In July the Coronation Committee, conscious that the queen was opposed to the idea, concluded that television cameras should be excluded from Westminster Abbey. Churchill was also opposed to its use (considering television vulgar), as was the Archbishop of Canterbury and the Abbey clergy. In particular the Church believed that viewers watching the ceremony over cups of coffee would make it a less dignified occasion. It was also thought that if the procession and service were on television fewer people would be on the streets. Instead, it was proposed, a film was to be made which would be shown (presumably suitably edited) to television viewers at a later date. The BBC, the only British television broadcaster at this time, was not consulted over the practicalities. Preconceived notions and misunderstandings over how the service could be shown live also contributed to the rejection of televising the ceremony at this stage.

There was, however, considerable parliamentary and public opposition to the announcement that the coronation would be broadcast on radio only. Consequently the issue was reviewed by committee, Cabinet and monarch. In early December the queen decided that the ceremony could after all be shown on television. Thereafter, after much discussion and compromise over exactly what was to be shown, the BBC, Buckingham Palace and Westminster Abbey were able to reach an agreement. The whole day would be given over to the procession and coronation service.

THE FIRST SUMMER

The Trooping of the Colour on 5 June, also known as the Queen's Birthday Parade, was the first great public occasion of the reign since the end of mourning. The colour trooped was that of the 2nd Battalion the Scots Guards. The queen rode Winston, a police horse, as she had done in 1951 when she had deputised for her father. The weather was better on this occasion, so much so that a guardsman fainted during the ceremony. There was also a Trooping of the Colour in Berlin at the (1936) Olympic Stadium. It was carried out by the 1st Battalion the Welsh Guards and the stadium, filled with some 40,000 people, was lined with the flags of the four occupying powers, the Dominions and overseas missions.

Later in June the queen attended Ascot and the opening of the Royal Tournament at Earls Court, London. Already an established feature of the London summer, the tournament had started in 1880.

The queen rides down the Mall on her way to the Trooping of the Colour ceremony, her first as queen, 5 June 1952.

Now in its sixty-second year, it offered an established programme with the already traditional competition between rival naval teams who raced 12-pounder guns over walls and across a 30-foot wide chasm. There was also a raid against 'enemy-held coastline' by Royal Marine Commandos. But there had been changes too, including the recent introduction of RAF police dogs and trick riding by despatch riders from the Royal Signals Training Centre at Catterick.

The first presentations at Court and royal garden parties were also held. Divorced people were not asked to the garden parties but divorcees were to be admitted to the coronation, given that (as the Earl Marshal put it) 'it is not Royal Ascot'. They were also present at the seventh Annual Royal Film Performance held towards the end of October. The film was a love story called *Because You're Mine*. It starred Mario Lanza in a story about an opera singer who became a soldier and won the sergeant's sister. Among those presented to the queen was Charlie Chaplin.

THE OTHER QUEENS

It was a couple of days after the late king's funeral that his widow formally announced that she would henceforth be called Queen Elizabeth the Queen Mother. But it was not until almost the end of Court mourning that she undertook her first official engagement. She flew to Fife on 13 May to inspect, as the regiment's Colonel in Chief since 1947, the 1st Battalion the Black Watch prior to its departure for the Korean War.

On 26 May Queen Mary was eighty-five, and for the first time a reigning monarch had her grandmother still living. On the eve of Queen Mary's birthday (her last) she revisited her birthplace, Kensington Palace, to examine the coronation robes worn by Queen Victoria. She thought they formed a suitable precedent for the new queen. Queen Mary was renowned for her knowledge and collection of antiques – often acquired without the owner's willing consent – and recast her will in 1952 so that it encompassed all she possessed and reflected her determination that all should be in order and (mostly) given to the new sovereign. Her hold on these – and life – remained: not long before her death (March 1953) she knew she was losing her memory but, as she told her friend Osbert Sitwell, she meant to 'get it back'.

THE QUEEN AND PARLIAMENT

The death of George VI and the accession of Elizabeth II led parliament to pass a new Civil List Act. The Civil List was (and still is) the payment from public funds to meet the expenditure arising from the queen's official duties. A select committee of the House of Commons was appointed in May and reported five weeks later. For the first time since 1837 provision had to be made for a queen regnant (as opposed to a queen consort). Unlike the payment to the consorts of kings, the provision for the Duke of Edinburgh was made from the Consolidated Fund, not from the Civil List.

In 1952 parliament decided that the annual Civil List should be fixed at £475,000. This compared with an annual payment of £410,000 for George VI which had, deliberately, been left unchanged since 1937. In 1952 the Labour opposition suggested ten-yearly reviews of the Civil List to take account of inflation. This was rejected by 239 to 211 votes. The Conservative government argued that such an approach would involve too much parliamentary scrutiny over the 'delicate' matter of royal finances. Instead there would be an annual minimum inflation allowance of £70,000 which would form a reserve in the early years of the reign to be drawn on later as inflation eroded the value of the original sum. Using surpluses in this way was a significant change, as it prevented them from being transferred to the monarch's personal wealth. The Chancellor of the Exchequer made clear to parliament that the queen would only pay tax on her private landed estates. All other sources of income, including the Civil List, would continue to enjoy tax exemption.

The Civil List Act specified an amount for each member of the royal family. For example, Princess Margaret was to continue receiving £6,000 a year; Queen Mary and the Queen Mother each received £70,000. Labour MPs failed in their attempts to reduce the provision made for the Queen, the Duke of Edinburgh and Princess Margaret. Under the Act, Civil List pensions, to the total value of £5,000 in any one year, were to continue. Among those who received such a pension in 1952 was Wyndham Lewis for his services to literature and art (£250).

On 4 November the queen opened her first parliament. The full traditional ceremony was followed, something which had not happened since 1938. For the first time photographs of the

Queen Elizabeth drives to her first state opening of parliament as monarch, November 1952.

procession of the Queen and Duke of Edinburgh through the Royal Gallery were allowed but none could be taken in the House of Lords itself. The queen wore the scarlet Parliament Robe of the young Queen Victoria. Before delivering the speech from the throne, Elizabeth made a formal declaration that she was a faithful Protestant and would maintain the Protestant succession.

There was some concern over the role and place of the Duke of Edinburgh in the State Opening. The duke had already caused some unease earlier in February when he had looked in briefly on a Commons sitting. Enoch Powell, a Conservative MP, told the prime minister that he should not appear in the chamber again. The duke did not return. As far as the State Opening of Parliament itself was concerned, the Lord Great Chamberlain, Lord Cholmondeley, concluded that it was best to follow the precedent established for Prince Albert – a chair of state. This was placed to the left of the throne but on a step lower than the throne itself. The consort's throne, which had been used by the Queen Mother, had already been taken to Lord Cholmondeley's country house. Despite pressure then (and subsequently) from Earl Mountbatten, the duke, although made a Prince of the United Kingdom in 1957, would not, unlike Albert, be given the courtesy title of Prince Consort.

Less than a week later, the queen led her first Remembrance Day ceremony.

Enoch Powell MP.

THE FIRST CHRISTMAS BROADCAST

The queen's first Christmas broadcast was live and for radio only. She refused to allow it to be televised; instead television showed a photograph of her at the microphone. The queen sat at the same chair and desk as those used by her father and grandfather. In her address she repeated the sentiments of her dedication to service which had first been heard in her Cape Town broadcast, as well as anticipating her forthcoming coronation. Other members of the royal family, including the Duke of Edinburgh, the Queen Mother and Queen Mary, gathered in a nearby room to listen to it.

Education and the World of Work

THE STRUCTURE OF EDUCATION

The structure of education in Britain was quite complex. Most pre-university education involved a mix of state and private (misleadingly known as 'public') schools. In 1952 education was free and compulsory for those aged between five and fifteen in the state sector, which was attended by over 90 per cent of children. There was talk at the beginning of the year (subsequently denied) that because of the prevailing economic difficulties, the government might limit compulsory schooling to those aged between six and fourteen. This did not happen. In addition to primary (for those aged between five and eleven years) and secondary (eleven to fifteen) education, there were some nursery places (for two to five year olds). Furthermore, about 3 per cent of those in state schools were over fifteen, mostly because they intended to go on to university. Over 10 per cent of this age group were in the private school sector.

The school leaving age had been raised to fifteen under the 1944 ('Butler') Education Act. Under that legislation, pupils were to be given an education appropriate to their 'age, abilities and aptitudes'. But in the absence of a national curriculum, it did not specify what this should be. The Act did ensure, however, that different forms of secondary education were available. These corresponded to and catered for the view that children's minds were of three types – abstract, mechanical and concrete. This resulted in the division into grammar, secondary technical and secondary modern schools respectively. Together they formed what was known as the tripartite system. The grammar school was to provide the professions, the technical school the crafts and the secondary modern the less skilled and service sector, such as retailing.

Selection was by examination in the last year of primary school – the eleven plus. The exam was a series of 'general intelligence tests'. Most people at this time still believed that it was possible to measure intelligence independently of social or environmental factors.

A cartoon of the time showed an older woman puzzled by the assessment. She is saying: 'I Q on my pore feet, not with me blinking 'ead' (spelling as in the original). About a quarter of those who sat the eleven plus passed it, although the government preferred to argue that no one failed, as the purpose of the exam was to identify the most appropriate form of secondary education. The result (whatever it was) showed this. The child only 'failed' if sent to the wrong type of school.

The intention was that the grammar school should be for children who hoped to reach university and for others with an academic bias. Its curriculum was a mix of the humanities, languages (including Latin and possibly Ancient Greek) and sciences. Pupils at grammar school stayed on until at least sixteen when they took the General Certificate of Education (GCE) at Ordinary ('O') Level. This was a single subject examination which was introduced in 1951 to replace the School Certificate, which represented success in a group of subjects. There were also single subject GCEs at Advanced ('A') and Scholarship ('S') Levels which were taught in the sixth form and which replaced the Higher School Certificate. Pupils sat eight or more GCE 'O' Levels and two or three 'A' Levels. Few sat 'S' Levels, and then normally only in one subject.

The secondary modern provided a lower level of general education with a practical bias. The curriculum was meant to be more closely related to the (perhaps presumed) interests, environment and ambitions of their pupils. The technical school was the smallest of the three with education there more directly focused on the needs of industry. Where appropriate, it took those who had only just failed to make it to grammar school. Even so, such a policy reinforced the idea that a technical education was inferior to an academic one. Only grammar school pupils in the state sector sat GCEs. However, it was expensive to provide all three types of secondary education and by the early 1950s Local Education Authorities (LEAs) preferred to offer just grammar and secondary modern schools. Parents too preferred to see more grammar schools being built in their area as it increased the chance of their children securing a place.

This secondary school system, however, was already under attack in 1952. Critics questioned how reliable the eleven plus was in identifying levels of ability, and maintained that as well as deciding the form of secondary education it also invariably determined the nature of subsequent adult employment and lifestyle. A child might show (in the words of the 1944 Act) high academic 'abilities' at the age of ten or eleven without having any marked 'aptitudes'. A child might have an 'aptitude' for a particular practical skill without

Maria MONTESSORI   RIP 1952

Montessori was a leading figure initially in Italian education. Born in 1870 she was first Italian woman to become a medical doctor. She lectured on what was then called 'pedagogical anthropology' and founded her first nursery school in an impoverished district of San Lorenzo. Her views in education were more child-centred and relaxed than those that generally prevailed at that time. Her schools became established throughout Europe and the USA. In 1912 she published *The Montessori Method* and in 1913 the first international course on her methods was held in Rome. She opened a teachers' training college in London in 1929. Five years later her work in Italy came to an end, as she was forced to close down all her activities there because of her pacifism. Operating for a while in Spain, she fled to India on the outbreak of the Spanish Civil War. In 1940 she was interned as an enemy alien in Madras but returned to Italy in 1947 to reorganise schools there.

intellectual ability. But the Act presumed that academic inability meant technical aptitude. Furthermore, there was little opportunity for redress or a second/later chance for those who did not make it to the grammar school at eleven.

The growing anxiety about the present form of the eleven plus, which in effect condemned three-quarters of children as 'failures' at the end of their primary school education, led some to wanting to change it and others to abandon it. There was the suggestion that an essay should be included in the assessment but this was seen as damaging to the 'neutrality' of intelligence tests. Miss G.M.B. Williams, President of the Association of Assistant Mistresses, went further at the Association's 1951/2 annual conference. She bemoaned the sole reliance on the eleven plus and argued that health, character, imagination and love of reading should also be taken into account in deciding a child's destination.

To have no exam or selection at all but instead one single all-in (or 'comprehensive') school was the other answer. Already by 1952 such a form of secondary education had been established in Windermere (1945) and Anglesey (1949). The planning of Kidbrooke, London's first purpose-built comprehensive school, was already in hand in 1952. It opened two years later.

GOVERNMENT AND EDUCATION

There were considerable extra demands on education in 1945 but insufficient good quality teachers or buildings to fulfil them. A campaign to remedy both shortcomings was undertaken by the

These under-eights demonstrate their height differences while playing 'ring-a-ring-a-roses', 1952.

postwar Labour government. In addition, between 1945 and 1952 the school population rose by about a million, partly because the school leaving age was raised in 1947 from fourteen to fifteen. To house, teach and provide school milk, school meals and school medical services for almost six million children in 1952 was quite a challenge.

But the government succeeded. There was a third of a pint of milk available each day for children who wished to have it, albeit attitudes towards its consumption would vary according to the weather. The milk could be lukewarm and perhaps 'going off' in summer, while it might be nearly frozen in the depths of winter. 'School dinners' were equally not always welcome but they formed an important part of many children's lives. The meals were normally prepared at the school and the price was subsidised (remitted in cases of need). Nearly half of LEA pupils had school dinners at this time. There was also free transport for children who lived more than a reasonable distance from their school. This was normally interpreted as over 2 miles for the under eights and over 3 miles above that age. Many young children enjoyed (and could safely undertake) the walk to school with their parent/friends, while older children might cycle.

The school medical service conducted medical examinations and vaccinations as well as some dental clinics and sun treatment for tuberculosis sufferers. It also investigated tendencies to rickets and growth disorders. But what most children of the time remembered was the visit by the nit nurse, sometimes known to an older generation as 'nitty Nora', who ruffled a child's hair and made grave pronouncements should anything be wrong. The medical room would display posters bestowing advice – in particular that 'coughs and sneezes spread diseases/trap them in your handkerchieveses'.

A schoolboy, doubtless the milk monitor, puts a straw in each bottle ready for break-time.

Primarily because of problems over the supply of materials, it was not until 1947 that LEAs could really begin to build new schools. Sites had to be found for the single-storey, long corridor school which was then the fashion but, given the emphasis on health and recreation, for large playing fields too. By the end of 1951 over 1,100 new schools were being built and most of these were to be in use a year later. The incoming Conservative government issued a 'stand-still' order which prevented the start of new school building projects for the following three months. In February 1952 Miss Florence Horsborough, the Minister of Education (but unlike her Labour predecessor not a member of the cabinet at the time), announced the closure of that year's educational building programme.

Teacher shortages had been reduced by encouraging men and women from the armed services to undertake an eleven-month course of study under the emergency training scheme which the Labour government had introduced. Service hospitals, camps and stately homes were used as additional teacher training colleges and some 35,000 men and women, mostly aged between twenty-one and thirty-five, entered the profession in the period following the war. The campaign to recruit teachers (especially women) continued into 1952.

SCHOOL LIFE

In general, primary education was mixed, both in terms of gender and (to a lesser extent) ability. Single-sex schools were a feature of much secondary education and grammar schools in particular streamed according to ability. As required under the 1944 Education Act there was a daily single act of worship which involved the whole school. It was held in the school hall and was often known as 'assembly'. Religious instruction was also taught – and was the only compulsory subject in the school curriculum. Both were predominantly if not entirely Christian in outlook, although parents could withdraw their children if they wished.

Discipline and respect for teachers were both emphasised. Punishment for misdemeanours might take the form of 'lines' – writing out a single statement ('I must not talk in class') a certain number of times. This might also be known as 'an imposition'. Pupils could also be kept in after school hours or during the lunch break ('detention'). For the most serious offences the cane could be used or, as a final resort, the miscreant expelled. Grammar schools had a prefect system drawn from the sixth form. They helped maintain discipline within the school but outside the classroom and could exact milder forms of punishment.

To enforce respect, in grammar schools at least, pupils would stand and collectively greet staff as they entered a classroom. Also staff would normally wear their university gowns. The academic nature of grammar school education was stressed too, with greater emphasis than elsewhere on the setting and following up of homework. Individual effort was encouraged through exams and a school prize (or speech) day which normally involved a guest with local or school links presenting books in acknowledgement of the successes of the previous year. Parents might also attend this event. Corporate identity within the school was encouraged through loyalty to a House. This was particularly called upon for the annual sports day. Overall school identity was developed through the

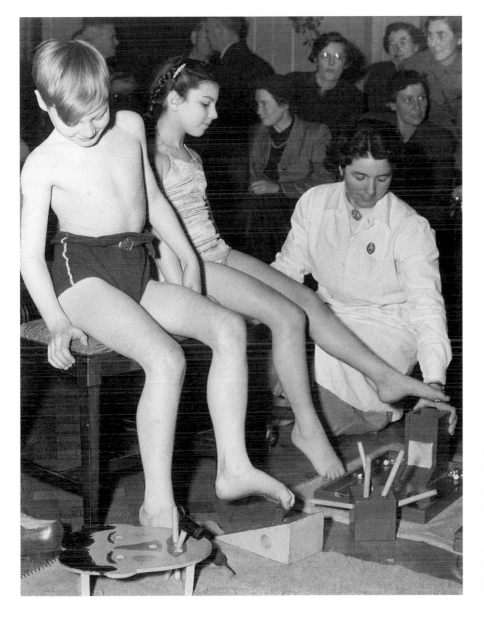

Berlie Stimson, nine, and Marie Milan, ten, use their feet to pick up small objects as part of a School Remedial Work Conference which suggested that minor physical defects were capable of turning into permanent deformities if not corrected in childhood. They are watched by a remedial worker from Oxford.

Empire Day Parade of Boy
Scouts in Danson Park, Bexley,
May 1952 (*Bexley Local
Studies and Archives Centre*).

wearing of uniforms, a school song and inter-school competitions. These were not necessarily limited to sports events as extra-curricular activities might include debating societies or quizzes. Hobby and interest clubs might also take place outside school hours.

National events rarely impacted on school life. Pupils were informed of George VI's death and for some that was the end of school for that day. As far as the king's funeral was concerned, the Minister of Education welcomed the idea of pupils gathering together and marking the occasion but did not think that it was necessary for schools to close. A few months later (24 May) was another national occasion – Empire Day.

Empire Day had been established in 1904 ostensibly to create a common sense of imperial unity and pride within all the territories. The date chosen was Queen Victoria's birthday. Such a history and purpose made it unacceptable to some Labour-controlled authorities, so its observance in Britain was patchy. But where it was celebrated, depending on the age of the children concerned, the day might involve a special assembly where the virtues of the Empire and British Commonwealth were extolled. There might be special songs, lessons on the institution's history/geography and a procession (perhaps with children in 'national costumes' from different parts of the Empire) around the playground or neighbourhood. Some schools belonged to the Empire Day Movement and copies of its magazine *New Empire* were distributed on this day.

SCHOOL BROADCASTS

Education was one of the three major obligations – the others were information and entertainment – contained in the BBC's first charter (1926). School radio broadcasts began soon afterwards and by 1952 the Corporation was making programmes for both primary and secondary schools. Over thirty series were broadcast in 1951/2. But this year also saw what was termed at the time as the 'experiment' of television broadcasts.

The idea of television broadcasts for schools had been under discussion since the late 1930s but there had been opponents from inside as well as outside the BBC – even to pilot schemes. In 1952 the Archbishop of Canterbury, who himself had been a schoolteacher, described the idea of television for schools as 'nothing less than a perfect disaster', believing that it would further separate pupil and teacher. But *The Times* was supportive. Originally planned for late 1951 or early 1952, the trial was delayed until May because the BBC's Outside Broadcast Unit was not available.

The first experimental television series for schools comprised twenty programmes (each between twenty and thirty minutes in length) on five groups of subjects. They were broadcast over four weeks to a few secondary schools in Middlesex on a special wavelength which was not normally used. The subjects included a modern dairy farm, people at work, visual explanations of scientific achievements (such as how an aeroplane flies) and unscripted discussions of topical subjects. In following up reactions, the verdict was encouraging although the 18-inch screen – the largest used – was thought to have been too small. In the autumn it was claimed that most LEAs were prepared to buy television sets for their schools. The Education Minister, however, stated that the current economic situation prevented the experiment from being developed further. The BBC did not resume school television broadcasts for some years.

HIGHER EDUCATION

There were over 80,000 students at British universities in 1952. This was a significant increase on interwar figures and most students were financed from public funds or scholastic endowments. There were fourteen degree-giving universities in England and Wales and four in Scotland. All were self-governing institutions. Although they

A researcher separates insects from soil samples by means of an array of funnels, University of Southampton, 1952.

received Treasury funding via the University Grants Committee the Ministry of Education had no formal jurisdiction over them. English universities in 1952 comprised Oxford, Cambridge, London, Birmingham, Bristol, Durham, Leeds, Liverpool, Manchester, Nottingham, Reading, Sheffield and Southampton. There was also the University of Wales. The four universities in Scotland were Glasgow, St Andrew's, Aberdeen and Edinburgh.

Southampton achieved independent university status in 1952, although its origins lay in the mid-nineteenth century and it had been made a university college in 1902. There were 900 under-graduates in 1952 and they could study for degrees in the arts, sciences, engineering, economics, education and the law. Its first chancellor was the Duke of Wellington. Other university chancellors at this time included Churchill (Bristol), Eden (Birmingham) and the Duke of Edinburgh (Wales and Edinburgh). The Chancellor of Oxford University was Earl Halifax and the Vice-Chancellor Sir Maurice Bowra. At that university in 1952 charters of incorporation were granted to Keble College and (the then) St Anne's Society, which was renamed St Anne's College. Cambridge's Chancellor was Lord Tedder. Early in the New Year Edinburgh installed Sir Alexander Fleming, the discoverer of penicillin (in 1928), as its rector while Aberdeen University also had a new rector. He was

James Keith O'Neill Edwards DFC MA – better known as Jimmy Edwards, the famous radio personality.

FURTHER EDUCATION

This was a thriving sector of education and the LEAs actively supported it. They could provide vocational and non-vocational courses in a variety of subjects and/or assist voluntary bodies and institutions to do so instead. As a result many communities could boast technical, commercial or art colleges and evening institutes. Evening classes were also organised by universities and such voluntary bodies as the Workers' Educational Association. There were now adult residential colleges which offered courses varying in length from a few days to a couple of weeks. Employers were encouraged to offer part-time release schemes to enable their workers to study in the day time.

THE STATE OF THE NATIONAL ECONOMY

The Second World War had harmed the economy through the loss of ships, damaged infrastructure (such as roads and railways) along with the consequences of changed production for, bomb damage to and delayed investment in industry. Some overseas assets had been sold to pay for war supplies (thereby reducing income from this source), while new debts had been incurred which brought with them increased (annual) debt repayments. The preoccupation with the war meant a fall in what Britain could earn abroad through exports. Such markets were not necessarily recovered when peace came. Rising import prices, especially of raw materials, added to Britain's problems.

The fundamental task for the British economy at this time was once again to earn more from overseas than it spent. The postwar years (including 1952) saw a sustained effort to achieve this through

---

Albert MANSBRIDGE   RIP 1952

A leading figure in British education, he founded the Workers' Educational Association (WEA). He was born in Gloucester in 1876 and educated at elementary schools and Battersea (London) Grammar School. After working as a clerk in London he joined the Co-operative Wholesale Society. On leaving school he attended evening classes and soon began to teach them too. In July 1903, after publishing articles on higher education for the working class, he founded the organisation which became known as the WEA. An early enthusiast for the association was William Temple (later Archbishop of Canterbury), who was its president from 1908 to 1924.

the use of purchase tax which was added to the selling price of items so affected. This reduced demand and raised revenue. There was also a mix of restrictions on industrial output for the home market and imports as well as controls on foreign currency exchange. Sterling had been devalued in 1949. But in 1952, excluding defence aid, the UK succeeded in converting the 1951 deficit of £414 million into a £148 million surplus. This was achieved primarily through reduced and lower priced imports; the value of exports increased mainly as a result of higher prices.

THE NATIONAL ECONOMY: A SECTOR ANALYSIS

Agriculture, forestry, fishing, mining and quarrying ('primary industry') together accounted for about 10 per cent of the British economy. In 1952 the government sought to reduce the previous year's level of imports by 10 per cent and looked to agriculture to play its part. As in years past, the government offered direct agricultural subsidies and guaranteed prices.

When the year opened Britain was in the middle of a foot-and-mouth epidemic which was believed to have been started by birds moving out of infected areas of continental Europe to the coastal areas of eastern and south-western England. Between November 1951 and June 1952 there were 430 outbreaks of the disease, and livestock worth £1.5 million was slaughtered. Outbreaks continued sporadically until the end of the year. Restrictions on livestock movements were imposed over wider areas and for longer than ever before. Many agricultural show societies cancelled their cattle, sheep and pig classes and attendances fell slightly below those of the previous year.

Nearly 30,000 people were employed in the fishing industry. The main fishing ports in England and Wales were Hull, Grimsby, Great Yarmouth, Lowestoft, Milford Haven and Fleetwood. Scotland's fishing centres included Aberdeen and the Moray Firth ports. London was the principal wholesale distributing centre and Billingsgate Fish Market (then near London Bridge) handled around 600 tons a day.

The most important of the primary industries was coal. It had been transferred to public ownership in January 1947 and was now run by the National Coal Board. The industry comprised 900 collieries in fifty areas and in 1952 employed 716,000 people (17,000 more than the previous year). The main coal-bearing areas were (roughly in order of output) Yorkshire, Nottinghamshire and Derbyshire, Durham and Northumberland, Central Scotland, South Wales, Lancashire and North Wales. Over 226 million tons of coal were produced, some of which was exported.

MANUFACTURING INDUSTRY

This was the largest single activity in the British economy, accounting for almost 40 per cent of gross domestic product. In terms of output and exports, the most important British industries were the metals and metal-users, textiles and chemicals. Metal and metal-using industries included iron and steel, vehicles, electrical engineering and machinery.

The steel industry had been nationalised in 1949 and was still under public control in 1952. It would return to private ownership (with some continuing government involvement) in 1953. Nearly half a million people were employed in the industry. New investment under way at this time included the Abbey Works at Margam (completed 1953) and Velindre. Both sites were in South Wales.

The vehicles industry made the largest single contribution to the export trade. Motor vehicles made up the most important group and

Grim evidence of the outbreak of foot-and-mouth disease which occurred this year. The sergeant is dipping his boots in disinfectant before leaving this farm in Lancashire.

A worker examines the sign proclaiming the nationalisation of the coal industry.

Britain was the largest exporter of such products in 1952, with the USA as the largest individual market by value for British cars. British car ownership was rising too, in part promoted by the Motor Show which was held each October at Earls Court. Many of the cars on display in 1952 were available for immediate delivery – the first time this was so since the 1930s.

Although over 700,000 cars were produced in 1952, some 4,000,000 bicycles were manufactured for export and home use. Malaya, India and Brazil were the largest overseas markets. Sales to America were increasing, particularly for lightweight bicycles which were popular with younger people. Bicycles were imported from Germany, France and Italy. Japan also supplied the market, their manufacturers sometimes using trade marks which could be taken for British ones.

The London Cycle and Motor Cycle Show was also held at Earls Court, soon after the Motor Show. One of the models on display cost less than £12 (including purchase tax) – the lowest postwar figure for an adult bicycle. Several companies also showed off their coronation models for 1953.

In 1952 Britain launched nearly a third of the world's new shipping tonnage and the industry employed over 200,000 people. Most ships were produced along the lower Clyde in Scotland and in north-east England along the lower reaches of the rivers Tyne, Wear and Tees; Merseyside, Barrow and Southampton were less important to the industry. Vessels built on the Clyde ranged from fast ocean-going vessels to cross-Channel steamers. The *City of Port Elizabeth* was completed towards the end of 1952. It was built by Vickers Armstrong for the Ellerman services to South Africa. It could accommodate 107 first class passengers, and many cabins included bathroom and toilet en suite. The extensive library, writing room and spacious dining room were all promoted as distinctive features. By way of contrast, at the beginning of the year a Shell oil tanker became the first merchant ship to be propelled by a gas turbine.

A Bristol saloon of the era.

This sector of the economy included the locomotive industry which was in two separate sections. The larger was involved in building and repairing locomotives and rolling stock for British Railways (also a recently nationalised industry). The smaller, privately owned section produced mainly for export. Locomotive building and repair by British Railways centred on Crewe, Swindon, Doncaster, Darlington, Derby, Eastleigh and Ashford. In all 210 steam engines were built for the nation's railways in 1952 – more than double the total number of diesel, diesel-electric and electric locomotives produced that year. British Railways was still clearly committed to steam as its main type of power but other forms of traction already existed on the network and new ideas were being investigated. Shortly before nationalisation, the Great Western Railway had ordered two turbine-electric locomotives, one from Switzerland (delivered in 1950) and the other from the Metropolitan-Vickers Electrical Company at Trafford Park, Manchester. Delivered in 1952, it was the first turbo-electric locomotive to be built in Britain. As Locomotive 18100 it was used on the London–Plymouth route. It could travel up to 90 mph and there were driver cabs at each end. Both locomotives, however, had been withdrawn from service by 1960.

CAR PRICES AT THE 1952 MOTOR SHOW

Bentley Continental £6,000 (export only; top speed 125mph; 16–21 mpg)

Aston Martin DB2 £2,723

Daimler £2,661

Jaguar XK120 £1,774

Rover £1,487

MG £989

Wolseley £997

Austin A40 Sports £913

Ford Zephyr £829

Vauxhall £833

Morris Minor £631

Austin 7 £553 (45 mpg)

1952 CLOTHES PRICES			
	£	s	d
Dress	3	5	11
Raincoat	3	19	6
Boy's suit	1	17	6
Man's suit	3	15	0
Coat	3	19	6
Skirt	1	3	11
Men's shoes	2	15	9

Distributive trades (predominantly retailing) formed the next largest sector in the economy and employed well over two million people. This was still the age of the independent shop as it handled more than half of the nation's retail trade. But this was the age too of the department store and variety chain store. The latter offered a wide variety of goods at low prices, avoiding when necessary brands subject to resale price maintenance (which specified the maximum price at which something could be sold) and usually without any clear division between different sections selling different goods. Customers were encouraged to handle the goods themselves as they were sold on open counters or in racks.

There were also about 1,100 retail co-operative societies. These were voluntary, non-profit-making associations engaged in retailing and controlled by their members who were also their customers. Any surplus was returned annually to members as a dividend. Dividends were proportionate to the value of most purchases made in the year: the member's number would be noted, along with the amount, at the time of each transaction. Although open to all, the co-op was particularly well supported by the working class (especially for food and clothing) who could rely on the quality and who welcomed the dividend (often called 'the divi') as an additional income. Returns on expenditure could be 10 per cent or higher.

BRITISH INDUSTRIES FAIR

This fair was first held in the autumn of 1914. It was originally designed to encourage home production of certain goods previously imported from Germany. In 1952 it took place at Olympia and Earls Court in London and West Bromwich, Birmingham. Among the highlights were some coronation souvenirs, including a miniature Coronation Chair in solid gold which included a removable model of the Stone of Scone. As a symbol of modernity, however, there was also a display promoting the Comet airliner. There was also a telephone on a stand with an amplifier so placed that it was possible to take down messages without holding the handpiece. The fair was visited by the Queen and Duke of Edinburgh soon after it opened.

THE NATIONAL WORKFORCE

The working population in 1952 was about 23 million – nearly 16 million men and 7.5 million women. The armed forces absorbed nearly 900,000 people and unemployment was around 2 per cent. At the beginning of 1952 total membership of British trade unions was 9,480,000. Most members were male – less than a quarter of female workers belonged to a union. Although there were 704 separate trade unions, the seventeen largest accounted for over two-thirds of trade unionists. Most unions were affiliated to the Trades Union Congress and there was a separate Scottish Trades Union Congress. Less than two million days were lost through strike action, half of which were in the mining, engineering and vehicle industries. Where workers were unable to organise themselves to protect their terms and conditions of employment, there were Wages Councils to safeguard their interests. There were many employers' organisations too, their central body being the British Employers' Confederation.

The standard minimum time rates for British manual workers varied between 2s 6d and 3s 6d per hour for men and 1s 9d and 2s 6d for women. Average weekly male earnings totalled £9 5s 11d; for a woman it was just over £5. The average for a farm worker was about £6 13s 2d while a miner received £12 6s 1d plus 11s 9d payment in kind (usually coal). The hours of work for women and young people between sixteen and eighteen were limited by law to forty-eight a week and for those under sixteen to forty-four. But normal hours of work were usually less and might be spread over five or five-and-a-half days. Overtime might also be worked. There were six statutory public holidays (two each at Christmas and Easter, Whit Monday and the first Monday in August), but most employees had at least one week's holiday with pay and the majority had at least two weeks. Other benefits of working at a particular place might be reduced/free access to the goods or services provided, a canteen with hot meals and clubs or sports facilities.

Equal pay for women continued to be an issue in both the public and private sectors. Those aiming to achieve this included the Equal Pay Campaign Committee (which had strong links with parliament and whose members at this time included Dr Summerskill and Lord Pethick-Lawrence) and the Equal Pay Co-ordinating Committee (a trades union pressure group). The most significant advance for women in this area in 1952 was the decision by the London County Council to introduce equal pay for its teachers.

Health and safety at work had high priority. There were Factory, Mines and Quarries Inspectorates, which encouraged the formation of Accident Prevention Committees and the appointment of Safety Officers at the nation's workplaces. The Ministry of Labour maintained a Safety, Health and Welfare Museum in London. The Royal Society for the Prevention of Accidents supported the Accident Prevention Movement, a voluntary educational group. Many employers exceeded the demands of the law in providing a doctor or industrial nurse on site. Even so there were over 1,600 fatal industrial injuries in 1952, including 472 in mines and quarries, 196 in railway service and 145 on ships registered in the UK.

Home Life and Leisure

THE IDEAL HOME – THE EXHIBITION

The twenty-ninth Daily Mail Ideal Home Exhibition was held at Olympia in March 1952. The exhibition centred around a series of gardens, houses and a village with seventeen shops. The theme of the gardens was music, which was provided by two quintets. There were fifteen gardens covering 2 acres. Among the features were wistarias (which were forced into flower in time for the exhibition), a topiary garden and an informal garden. A waterfall splashing over mossy rocks into a pool and a Scottish packhorse bridge over a mountain stream completed this idyll and were particularly popular.

The village green with shops was a new idea for the exhibition. The green itself boasted the 500-year-old stone pillar from the village of Meriden, Warwickshire. Located roughly midway between Birmingham and Coventry, this village was said to mark the exact centre of England.

The six houses included examples constructed by private enterprise and the 'People's House', a term coined by the Minister for Housing and Local Government (and future prime minister) Harold Macmillan. The houses were in a Georgian style with two or three bedrooms. Macmillan sought to popularise the People's House through encouraging widespread interest in it, especially from local authorities and would-be occupants. Among the features of the People's House was a black lustre firegrate which was slow burning and (to quote the phrase of the time) 'would stay in all night'. It was Macmillan too who named and promoted the 'Old People's House'. This was a bungalow designed to give an elderly couple independence and privacy. Given their likely weaker physical state, the furniture was raised higher above the ground to make brushing and dusting easier.

THE IDEAL HOME – THE HOUSING REALITY

A view from the 1952 Ideal Home Exhibition.

The most desperate and perhaps the most significant of all the post-war shortages was housing. The minister responsible for dealing

Harold Macmillan, the Minister of Housing and Local Government, makes a speech to mark the official opening of six new houses at Ruislip in March 1952. These houses were built by non-traditional methods and finished in a mere seven weeks.

with this in the new Labour government had been Nye Bevan, who had not only established the National Health Service but oversaw the house-building programme too. For a variety of reasons his policy was to promote local authority housing for rent (often known as council housing). When Labour left office in 1951 less than 20 per cent of houses built since the war had been for owner-occupiers. The incoming Conservative government had different priorities and under its Minister of Housing the party's ambition for Britain to be a 'property-owning democracy' began to become a reality. Churchill made the appointment on condition that he built 300,000 houses a year. This was not quite the case in 1952 but the target was reached in each of the subsequent six years.

In January 1952 Harold Macmillan had already opened two 'people's houses' at Desford near Market Bosworth in Leicestershire. They were built for £970 in twelve weeks for the local rural council and the weekly rent was 12s 6d (excluding rates). For this the tenants enjoyed three bedrooms, a bathroom, a separate toilet, a living room, a dining annexe and a kitchen. Macmillan spoke of such houses as 'pioneers'. Even so the high marriage rate in the years following the end of the war meant that for most of the decade (let alone 1952 itself), many young couples started married life living with their parents, usually the bride's.

But once in their own home life could and often did become better. Utility furniture, which had, at least in the immediate postwar period, limited the nature and design of furniture produced, ceased

A Courts furniture exhibition.

to be made soon after the Conservatives took office. New ideas and new materials were beginning to be taken up and new technology gradually transformed the home, at least for some.

In 1950 the Council of Industrial Design issued a folio of contemporary designs in wallpaper, including papers produced by such companies as Coles, John Line, Sandersons and Shand Kydd. In 1951 John Line produced the first screen-printed British wallpapers. They featured at the Festival of Britain, as did designs using the new technique of microphotography. Wallpapers were still printed with patterns called 'Insulin' and 'Boric Acid'. Although linoleum ('lino') also continued to be a feature in many people's homes, there were now also thermoplastic floor tiles which were marketed as 'easy-wipe', as was the plastic laminate Formica. This had been developed in the 1940s but was only now beginning to transform homes. To begin with this colourful, heat-resistant laminate was only available as a flat sheet: an edging piece had to be glued on. The joins were covered with metal or plastic strips. It was often used to replace wood or enamelled surfaces and was particularly suitable for use in the kitchen, although as the decade proceeded it was also to be deployed elsewhere in the house.

THE KITCHEN

In practically all homes in 1952 the kitchen was seen as 'the woman's domain'. Many women continued to take pride in their domestic responsibilities which centred around what went on here. While they did not necessarily want to 'get out of the kitchen' the appeal of devices marketed as 'labour-saving' was increasingly great and the opportunity to acquire them growing. In the interwar years many middle-class homes had often had earlier versions and/or had day or live-in domestic help. Now any household with a 'woman who does' was likely to employ her outside the kitchen.

Even more significant by the early 1950s, although it was to become even more apparent as the decade progressed, was that what had previously been seen as middle-class luxuries in the home were fast becoming working-class necessities. With almost full male employment and increasing (if part-time and lower paid) work for married women, together with (albeit restricted) hire purchase facilities, this part of the home in particular could easily become 'modern'. The goal for many in 1952 was the English Rose kitchen. This offered a completely fitted kitchen and incorporated appliances and fitments. It included fitted electric cooker, double sink and laminated furniture. It was available in single units too. Colour schemes for 'modern' kitchens were pastel walls and strong colours

Many houses remained unmodernised at this time, as this Bristol scullery photographed in the 1950s shows. The only modern touch is the packet of Tide washing powder on the window-sill.

(red, yellow and blue) for the plastic laminated worktops. This was because colour pigments were expensive and the paints most readily available were in pastel colours.

There was also the popular multi-purpose cabinet. These wooden pieces of furniture were either left in their natural state or painted. Behind a dropped down or pull-out enamelled flap would be found a series of shelves and compartments. They might also include storage jars and ventilation grilles for storing fresh food. But the refrigerator was also entering many homes at this time.

Frigidaire, an American company, had started manufacturing electric refrigerators in Britain in 1923. There were also gas-operated refrigerators. Both continued to be a feature of 1952, with

Thanks to Mr Therm . . . he's giving her

the perfect gift . . .

CHEAP HOT WATER
BY GAS!

An instantaneous gas water heater is the *perfect* present for any housewife—it gives her the luxury of instant hot water, at a tap's turn, *for a very non-luxury price.* Everyone can afford the joy of instant hot water in kitchen or bathroom with gas water heaters. See the full range—at really reasonable prices—in Mr. Therm's new Hot Water Parade at your Gas Showrooms *NOW.* Easiest of easy terms available.

£1 DISCOUNT OFFER!

Buyers of new gas water heaters will receive a special £1 discount if they trade in their old heaters.

ONLY GAS CAN GIVE YOU INSTANT HOT WATER ENDLESSLY

MINIMAIN 60
Instantaneous sink water heater. Handy and really low-priced. For sinks or basins.

EWART S.140 AV
Fully automatic instantaneous bath water heater. Serves bath and adjacent basin.

Gas-hot water is cheap, quick, reliable!

SOUTHERN **GAS** SERVICE

the latter promoted by 'Mr Therm', a symbol of the gas industry. But Electrolux offered them too, with the slogan 'the flame that freezes'. Separate 'deep freeze' (originally the trade name of another American company) facilities in the home were not known at this time either in the USA or in Britain, although fridge-freezers were already being made in America. A 'family' Frigidaire cost almost £100 and offered over 4 cubic feet of inside storage space. Promotional literature stressed that it was cheap to run and extolled the benefits of 'once a week shopping', permitting more leisure time. For those yet to acquire this appliance, there was always the larder. This was usually situated on the north or east side of the kitchen and often had a stone/tiled floor and shelves. Small units with wire-mesh doors might be used for storing meat.

There were changes too in the way food was cooked. Although housewives had developed methods to test for temperature (such as how quickly greaseproof paper changed colour) many wanted to replace the 'low', 'medium' and 'high' knobs on their cookers with thermostatic controls, which were now an established feature. Thermostats had first been used in gas ovens in 1923 and in electric ovens in 1938. Having hot food instantly available was also sought-after before the days of automatic timers and microwaves. One solution was the vacuum flask. Thermos was so successful that, like Hoover, the company name became the generic name for this product. In 1952 Thermos promoted the idea of cooking supper in the morning and preparing breakfast (porridge, coffee) the night before. Such was the demand for (or perhaps more accurately the problems over supply of) flasks that, according to one advertisement at this time, customers were urged to 'keep asking for them'.

Other conveniences already on the market included the washing machine, electric food mixer, dishwasher and potato chipper. But few homes had them. Less than one in six households, for instance, had a washing machine in 1952 (even though they could be rented) and most of these were little more than wash boilers. Wringing was done by hand. The spin dryer and, a little later, the twin-tub both belonged to the mid-1950s.

G.E.C.

The name to remember
for all electric
appliances in the home

As most household fabrics were cotton or linen, boiling was generally considered to be the best way of keeping laundry clean and fresh. Many housewives still used a mix of washing soda and grated ordinary soap, but soap powder was well established with Persil, Rinso, Tide and Oxydol being among the most popular. Other brands were Dreft, Lux and Paddy, the last a speciality of the soap works owned by the Co-operative Wholesale Society. Like the other two, it was something of a luxury item, being normally used only for hand washing silks and woollens. There were also soapless detergents for the weekly wash. These were still very new for 1952 and were not made from traditional fats and alkali.

SHOPPING

Rationing was still in force in 1952. This meant that the consumer was restricted to a fixed quantity of each rationed food for a fixed period. Most people were on ordinary rations, but there were special allowances for certain invalids, expectant mothers and vegetarians. Instead of meat and bacon, vegetarians received a special allowance of cheese and extra vegetable margarine. Underground coal miners were allowed extra meat. Consumers registered with a retailer for each rationed food. The amounts of the rations varied with changes in supplies. In 1952 the foods so controlled were meat, bacon (except cooked gammon), tea, sugar, butter, margarine and cooking fats, cheese, eggs, sweets and chocolate. The meat ration fluctuated during the year but there were increases in price too – partly because of the reduction in government food subsidies. In August the butter ration was reduced by one ounce a week and the margarine ration was increased by the same amount. This meant that the total ration of fats was unchanged at nine ounces per person per week. The cheese ration was reduced from one and a half ounces to one ounce per person. It had once been eight ounces per week and had not been this low since June 1941. Tea came off rationing in October 1952.

Some of the new/substitute foods such as spam continued to supplement the traditional diet but, with few regrets, snoek was no longer available in 1952 – at least not for human consumption. Introduced after the war and off points from 1949, this fish never became the housewife's favourite. Ten million tins had been imported from South Africa and most, by the early 1950s, were being sold as a special treat for cats.

Food shopping still involved visits and often queues at several different, specialist outlets – the butcher, baker and (if not now the candlestick maker) the grocer. Food chains such as the Co-op, Tesco

---

1952 GROCERY PRICES

Goods were sold in pounds (lb) and ounces (oz); 16oz made 1lb (equivalent to 0.45kg). Liquid was measured in pints (a pint was equivalent to 0.568 of a litre) and there were eight to a gallon.

Potatoes	2d per lb
butter (rationed)	4s per lb
milk	7d per pint
meat (rationed)	2s per lb
tea	2s 6d per lb
Ovaltine	1s 6d, 2s 6d and 4s 6d

and Sainsburys were already well established by mid-century but were undergoing changes in the way in which they operated. Sainsburys opened its first modernised store on 23 February 1950 at Selsdon near Croydon in Surrey. This involved substantial redevelopment of a large existing branch incorporating such new ideas as fluorescent lighting and perspex. It also had plate glass instead of open windows and the central shutters were replaced with permanent doors. But above all there was self-service. This method of selling had been tried in a small way in some London Co-ops but the Selsdon Sainsburys branch was a more significant (and, as it turned out, pioneering) venture.

How to shop in one of the new self-service stores.

The company's first purpose-built self-service shop was opened on 25 February 1952 on the site of the bombed-out Eastbourne shop. Such branches were generally welcomed by customers who liked the chance to choose items at leisure and actually see what was in stock rather than queue frustratedly and then enquire. On entering the store people were greeted with 'prams' – metal frames on wheels that could accommodate two wire baskets. There were also refrigerated cabinets and air-cooled counters which allowed perishable foods to be kept chilled. Only a few customers found fault with the new system. Some felt that they had become something akin to shop assistants and others were annoyed that they had chosen more goods than they had originally intended!

EATING

Three meals a day served at the same time and involving most (preferably all) of the family was an established part of daily life for many, although by no means all, in 1952. Despite the existence of school meals and works canteens many working-class people (in particular) preferred to make their way home for the midday meal, which might be known as dinner. For various reasons, fewer middle-class men came home for lunch. Their wives enjoyed the longer break which the husbands' absence offered but, following an afternoon rest and some social activity, would ensure that the main meal was on the table for their husbands' return.

Sunday dinner/lunch was considered the best meal of the week and everyone still living at home was expected to attend and sit round the table with the rest of the family. Married children might

visit that day but would normally come for tea. Only a minority of homes would invite guests to a main meal (except at Christmas). Preparation for the main meal would, as usual, be the responsibility of the woman, who might also wish to combine this with morning worship. Although there might be some help from the husband, the morning for him was more likely to involve staying in bed longer, washing the car, visiting friends or the public house, or leisure activities such as sport or gardening. There were over a million allotments in 1952 and Percy Thrower's helpful article 'How to make a compost heap' appeared in a November issue of *The Listener*.

Certainly, other than bread, most meals would be predominantly home cooked, including own garden produce. The convenience foods of the time were mainly limited to tins with a few frozen items – the latter, however, could be quite expensive for most people and were difficult to store. Significantly advertisements for Wall's ice-cream highlighted the point that it solved the 'sweet problem' and, provided it was wrapped up well in newspaper when bought,

A grocer's shop, 1950s. The grocer would have known the customer's name and probably offered delivery of her 'order'. She is holding her ration book (*Bromley Central Library*).

would stay firm for two to three hours, by which time it would be just right for eating.

There might also be late afternoon/early evening tea. The nature of the meal would depend on what else featured that day to eat. It might be some or all of sandwiches (sweet or savoury and sweet), tinned fruit, scones and cake. There might also be something 'tasty' (normally cooked) which was moving the meal towards 'high tea'. The day usually closed with tea or a milk drink such as Horlicks, which was designed to ward off 'night starvation'.

RADIO

The single most important source of information and entertainment in the home was the radio. In 1952 almost 11.25 million sound-only licences were issued at £1 each. There were three BBC radio stations – the Home Service, the Light Programme and the Third Programme. While the first two stations broadcast throughout the day, the Third went out in the evenings only and had the smallest regular audience. At that time too people also tuned in to overseas stations, occasionally for concerts but more normally to Radio Luxembourg for a lighter diet of music. Unlike the BBC at this time, Radio Luxembourg mainly offered popular music including a hit parade which it had re-introduced in 1948.

Radio's ability to reach the nation on special occasions was already over a generation old in 1952. The BBC provided extensive

These two nurses seem quite happy chatting and listening to the radio.

coverage of events between the death and funeral of George VI, merging the three stations and altering schedules accordingly. The most popular aspect of its broadcasting was entertainment and sport which this year included the Olympics.

Two programmes had become essential listening for many of the population: *Mrs Dale's Diary* and *The Archers*. Both were an established part of many people's lives, and Mrs Dale being 'worried about Jim' was already becoming something of a catchphrase. The same could be said about some of the comments which featured in another programme of the time – *The Goon Show*. This had first been broadcast (under the title *Crazy People*) in May 1951. The stars in the second (1952) series included Peter Sellers, Harry Secombe, Spike Milligan and Michael Bentine, with characters such as Major Bloodnok and Neddy Seagoon. Phrases associated with the programme included 'He's fallen in the water'.

Another popular programme of the time was *Take It From Here*. Written by Frank Muir and Dennis Norden, it was first broadcast in 1947 and, following some modification, was extremely popular by 1952. By that time it was a mix of variety and (in effect) a serial evolving around the life of the Glum family. This comprised Mr Glum (Jimmy Edwards), his son the hopeless Ron (Dick Bentley) and Ron's long-suffering fiancée Eth (Joy Nichols).

Tony Hancock was beginning to hit the airwaves too when he was hired to play tutor to ventriloquist Peter Brough's dummy in *Educating Archie*. Another popular programme was *One Minute Please*, the forerunner of the similarly named *Just a Minute*. But radio was not all comedy. This year, for instance, the Light Programme broadcast Edgar Lustgarten's crime series *Prisoners at the Bar*.

TELEVISION

In 1952 the BBC, with its one channel (405 lines), was the nation's only provider of television. During the course of the year transmitters at Kirk o'Shotts and Wevenoe, in Wales, were opened. Consequently from late summer that year television was available to almost 80 per cent of the population but was owned by under 20 per cent (less than 1.5 million licences), the majority of whom were working class. But this situation was changing rapidly. About 800,000

A family watches television, which was just beginning to catch on in the early 1950s. (*Manchester Central Library*)

television sets were produced in Britain during this year which saw, for the first time, television sales exceed those of radio. This was achieved even though purchase tax on the former was 66.6 per cent and there were hire purchase restrictions.

A combined sound and vision licence cost £2 – twice the cost of a sound-only licence. Television detector vans were developed this year to ensure that those people who needed a licence actually had one. Although there were television programmes every day, broadcasting hours were relatively few and not continuous and some programmes were in sound only.

Television Newsreel, which had started in January 1948, was the most popular programme and was now broadcast five times a week. It provided news of the nation and the world. *About Britain*, a new programme for 1952, focused on national life. This typified the Corporation's attempt, in view of the growing audience outside the capital, to present programmes of interest to the nation as a whole. Hence the launch this year of *Special Enquiry*. Among the topics investigated were housing and employment. But probably the most discussed programme was *What's My Line?* with Gilbert Harding. Outstanding productions of the year included *Nineteen Eighty-Four*, *Dial M for Murder* and *Anastasia*. The Children's Television Department had been set up in 1950 and *Watch with Mother* was broadcast from Monday to Friday from 3.45 to 4.00. Programmes featured then included *Muffin the Mule* (with Annette Mills) and *Andy Pandy*.

LEISURE OUTSIDE THE HOME: WOMEN

The dual impact of technology and smaller families increased the time available to women to pursue their own interests. There were many opportunities to spend time constructively with others in a similar position – which might be church based (for example the Mothers' Union) or not. Two organisations – both established in Britain before the Second World War – which were particularly well supported at this time were the Townswomen's Guilds and the Women's Institutes (WI). Although both were overtly non-political, they played an important role in raising the skills and wider awareness of their members and campaigned on many issues which mattered to them and their communities. At the 1952 WI annual meeting, for instance, particular reference was made to the need for improved water and electricity supplies in the country. It also drew attention to child neglect (urging members to report instances which they might encounter) and the danger of the sale of certain types of comics and their effect on young minds. As part of WI members' development of their own minds, Denman College had been established a few years earlier offering in particular short-stay residential education.

LEISURE OUTSIDE THE HOME: MEN

With most men in full-time employment working a five and a half day week, entertainment outside the home was mostly local. Indeed, that was the term ('local') used to describe the public house which any man and (to a considerably lesser extent) any woman might patronise. Hence customers were also known as patrons. But television sets were also beginning to make an appearance in public houses in order to retain or invite custom which might otherwise look elsewhere or stay at home. 'The day the television came' altered the man's lifestyle as much as anyone else's in the home, but in 1952 the losses for the local (and for sport) were relatively small.

Sport continued to be important for many men, both as spectators and participants. Although mainly associated with Saturday afternoons, there were mid-week activities too. This applied not only to football and rugby, but also to motor-cycle dirt track racing (speedway) and greyhound racing which were both particularly popular at this time and often took place in the same stadium. Supporters might also combine their interest in a sport with a bet.

Betting in 1952 was controlled by a mix of common, municipal and national law. Credit betting off-course with a licensed bookmaker was legal, as was using ready money for a bet on course. This was

FOR HOME CONSUMPTION

Gilbey's port	18s
	9s 6d a flask
Gordon's gin	£1 13s 9d
VAT 69 whisky	£1 15s
Wills' Whiffs	3 for 1s 10d
(small cigars)	6 for 3s 7½d
Philip Morris	3s 9d for 20
(cigarettes)	
Minors	2s 8d for 20
(cheap cigarettes)	

the main reason for greyhound racing's popularity. But most bets were for cash and off-course, and therefore were illegal. Even so, street betting was widespread in most working-class communities, with the bookies concerned employing 'watchers' to raise the alarm or mislead the police.

Football pools were the other form of mass betting. As many as three families in every four in some communities would spend Wednesday evening together in order to be able to fill in the football coupon(s). Around half of all postal orders bought at this time were for enclosing with football pool entries.

LEISURE OUTSIDE THE HOME: THE FAMILY

Going to the cinema was the most popular leisure activity outside the home. Attendances had peaked in 1946 when it was estimated that one-third of the British population had gone to the cinema at least once a week. Thereafter attendances had begun to fall, although the rapid collapse in audience figures and extensive closures of picture palaces occurred after 1952.

Although all ages and both sexes went to the cinema, as in previous years the greatest support came from those in towns and in the working class, especially in Scotland. Children and adolescents made up a significant proportion of attendance figures, in particular with the popularity of Saturday morning pictures (where it was not unknown for a child, having bought a ticket, to open the emergency exit and admit friends free). But school and local cinema clubs also thrived. Women at home might attend a matinee, perhaps combining it with afternoon tea which some cinemas still offered and served on a separate floor.

Programmes would normally comprise two films, trailers for forthcoming films and a newsreel. There were also news cinemas which only showed newsreels. Less common than in the past was some form of live entertainment such as a talent show or musical recital – the days of the wurlitzer were almost over. Cinema performances would close with the playing of the National Anthem. Audience responses to this differed (especially if there were a particular tram or bus to catch) but most people remained to listen to and stand for it.

The growth in car ownership was also to affect family leisure. In 1948 there were almost two million private motor cars and vans on Britain's roads. By 1952 there were over three million. This represented about one car for every seven families and ownership was now rapidly extending to the working class despite the high level of purchase tax and hire purchase (HP) restrictions which

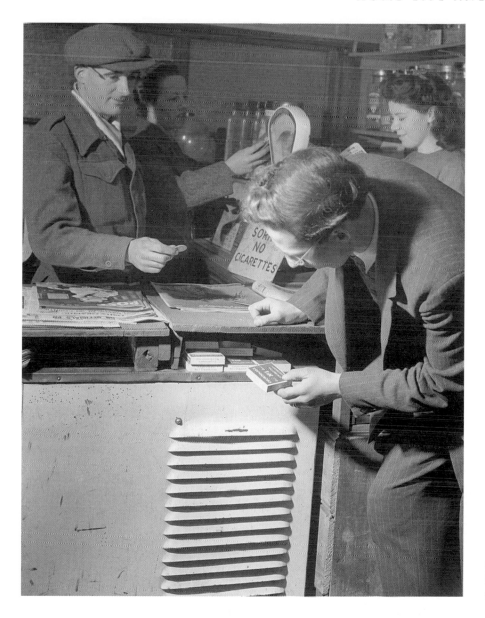

Despite the sign on display there appears to be a supply of cigarettes under the counter!

prevailed. That said, as in the 1930s, the second-hand market was also important, especially for the first-time purchaser. The annual road fund licence was levied but people often chose to pay for less than a year, laying their vehicles up during the winter months. There were speed limits in towns, and motorists were having to get used to pedestrian crossings. Belisha beacons had appeared in the 1930s and were already familiar. There were no speed restrictions on the open road, nor were vehicles subject to regular safety checks.

There was, however, some anxiety over the consequences of drinking and driving. There was a joint investigation by the Bristol University Department of Psychology and the Medical Research Council. They wanted to identify how much alcohol people could imbibe before becoming incapable of driving safely. Volunteer students were given free drinks and asked to drive in a device which simulated driving along a road at up to 70 miles an hour. Volunteers were not told whether the liquid they consumed contained alcohol or not. The tests were expected to take up to a year.

Although people might travel to work in cars, motorists normally used their vehicles for convenience and leisure – most notably (after washing it earlier that day) for the Sunday afternoon run out to the country. Cyclists and walkers went along too, and the countryside could be quite crowded that day, especially if a visit to a stately home were involved. Significantly, the National Trust's membership increased from just over 28,000 in 1951 to almost 36,000 in 1952 – its biggest numerical rise to date.

The seaside remained a popular destination too for both cars and other forms of transport, whether for a day or longer. Railway excursions to the seaside continued to be run (the network ran an additional 2,000 trains over Easter 1952) and were well supported. But nationally speaking, by 1952 less than half of the holidaymakers in Britain arrived by train. Bus companies, helped by the end of

Butlin's Holiday Camp at Bognor Regis, quite recovered from its wartime role as a military training centre.

petrol rationing and increases in permitted vehicle sizes at the start of the decade, secured a growing share of the market. There was a greater willingness among passengers to travel overnight. By 1952 places to which it was now possible to travel non-stop from London included Ilfracombe, Weymouth, Torquay, Brixham, Minehead, Lynton, Newquay and Swanage. The year also saw holiday interest in another form of coach – the return of the camping coach. The Western Region offered a coach that could accommodate up to eight people. Such coaches were to be found at selected stations for a weekly rental of between £7 and £10.

Most of those who holidayed in 1952 did so in Britain and its seaside resorts were still the preferred destinations – but not for much longer. Jugs of tea from a small beach hut, trips around the bay, brass bands on the seafront, slot and speak-your-weight machines as well as the end of the pier show itself were all beginning to pale for some. The early 1950s marked the last great age of the British seaside resort. It was a Victorian invention as far as its development and appearance were concerned, despite the investment which some resorts had made in the interwar period, and people were soon to look elsewhere. There was some evidence of this already in the form of the holiday camp and overseas package holidays.

A row of chalets at Butlin's Clacton camp.

The holiday camp first emerged as a commercial enterprise in the 1930s, notably under Butlin and Warner. Billy Butlin in particular was to develop the camp further after the Second World War with Clacton, Filey and Skegness all opened within a short time. By 1952 those holidaying at such camps accounted for 3 per cent of holidaymakers. The package holiday can be said to date from May 1950 when some twenty people paid a newly founded and still small company called Horizon £35 10s each for a two-week holiday in Corsica – under canvas! More conventional accommodation at Amalfi or Salerno in southern Italy would have cost about £80.

People were already being encouraged to take their car overseas with the inauguration of the car ferry service in the summer. Operating between Dover and Boulogne, SS *Lord Warden* had a turntable which enabled cars to be swung round and returned along one side of the vessel ready for driving off through folding steel doors at the stern. Remarkably, the vessel could also accommodate coaches and double-decker buses.

Wherever people took their holiday there was normally a sense of sadness as they began the journey home. But, according to some of the advertisements of the time, there was anxiety too. 'Can you lock up for the night or leave your flat (or house) empty without fear of being burgled?' This was an advertisement for a leading safe manufacturer. Readers were invited to send for an illustrated booklet entitled *How a burglar works – and how to stop him*.

FASHION AND DRESS FOR WOMEN – HAUTE COUTURE

The high fashion industry – in terms of seasonally presented, designer-led fashions – was almost a hundred years old in 1952. Founded in Paris, it took its origins from the British-born Charles Frederick Worth and Otto Bobergh. It was they who decided on the leading role of the designer when they established their fashion house in 1868. Previously the clients had determined the dictates of fashion. Worth, a former fabric salesman at the London department store of Swan & Edgar, was successful and his approach attracted others to Paris to set up houses in a similar way. In Britain the top end of the fashion trade until the early twentieth century was dominated by Court dressmakers. The fashion designer's links with monarchy continued to be important in the postwar period. Hardy Amies dressed the queen in 1952 while Norman Hartnell was to be responsible for her embroidered coronation gown.

The New Look had been introduced by Christian Dior in 1947. It created an international sensation and, although it underwent change, was still influential in 1952. Dior, along with Balmain and Balenciaga, dominated the couture scene in that year. Yet it was to be enlivened by two newcomers – Hubert de Givenchy (Paris) and John Cavanagh (London). Michael of Lachasse also launched two lines that made quite an impact at the time – the gaucho, which was described as a big bold short-coat, and the masher, which was a narrow boxed jacket with an Edwardian look.

The models themselves were beginning to become household names. This was the era of Fiona Campbell Walter, Bronwyn Pugh, Barbara Goalen and Anne Gunning. In February 1952 *Picture Post* described Barbara Goalen as Britain's number one fashion model and gave an account of her forthcoming one-woman world tour. This would take in 40,000 miles in four weeks – and she would take with her twenty-six suits and dresses. The tour was sponsored by textile manufacturers. Mrs Goalen, a widow, had begun modelling in 1948

These models are wearing jeans – a far cry from their birth as working clothes and almost as distant from today's version.

for economic reasons (she had two young children). She was credited with introducing the 'doe-eyed' look which was achieved by a thick line of kohl making the eyes look large and startled.

If the leading names in fashion in the early 1950s were Dior and Balenciaga, one of the main issues of discussion in 1952 was, to use a phrase coined at the Paris spring collection of that year, 'the wandering waistline'. Dior still favoured the high waist while Balenciaga adopted slack-waisted dresses and what were termed middy-line suits. Other leading fashion accoutrements/issues were boleros, spencers, minute hug-me-tights, deep yokes with pleating breaking from them to form an entire dress, and various uses of belts.

Coats narrowed from those which had appeared in earlier seasons and skirt lengths dropped an inch or two (eleven and a quarter being the most fashionable) towards the ground. Fur had been a luxury item, not least because of the 100 per cent purchase tax. When this was cut then fur began again to be used for collars, cuffs and pockets, as well as for muffs, stoles and capes.

The New Look had led to a fashion for large hats which went well with the full skirts of the period. But hats changed style too, with

the bathing-cap design the most significant. Other women wore hats best described as flat top-of-the-head pancakes and modified pill-boxes. Melusine – a soft furry hat fabric – was particularly popular. Simone Mirman, who opened her own salon in 1947, received her first royal commission in 1952 when she was asked to create a choice of hats for Princess Margaret.

Evening dresses were either day length, with perhaps a camisole top covered by matching bolero, or short dancing dresses with bouffant skirts falling to about ten inches from the ground. These were often worn at weddings by bridesmaids or even the bride. Stoles were much in evidence, the latest being ring stoles (just shoulder width), and were available in every fabric from fur to lace.

The fabrics used this year were indeed a mix of old and new. Tweeds, especially black and white, were popular in the autumn, while chiffon, crepe and lace were deemed to have made something of a comeback. The leading colours were grey (especially the darker shades), greens, sherry, turquoise and white. White was especially popular and was used for jackets, coats and hats. Shoes became even lighter than the previous year and were often held to the foot by delicate straps.

OFF THE PEG

With the end of clothes rationing and utility designs, manufacturers began to produce clothes in all price ranges. These were sold through high street shops and department stores. The main differences between the expensive and cheaper versions were the fabrics used and the nature of the cut. The style was not an issue as couturier designs could be copied and mass produced. Indeed, in 1951 Balmain had opened branches in the USA selling ready-to-wear clothes which had been adapted from his designs to suit the American market.

School uniforms in 1952 were still the gymslip and blouse. Calf-length trousers were usually worn when teenage girls went cycling. Trousers, although such a feature of female wartime wear, were now more associated with leisure than with work, slim-fitting rather than straight-legged. Holiday wear was more relaxed with girls' skirts above the knee and shorts on the beach or for games. Swimsuits were often made of bright cotton fabric. They were

gathered up with shirring elastic to fit closely. The bikini costume (which appeared in 1946 and was named after the atomic bomb test on the atoll of the same name) had first been seen on British beaches at the start of the decade. It too was a sensation, particularly later in the fifties after being popularised by Brigitte Bardot.

FASHION AND DRESS FOR MEN – HAUTE COUTURE

There was no designer-led equivalent in the late 1940s of the New Look for men. In 1952 wealthy clients patronised Savile Row tailors who would work to their specifications. But there was soon to emerge a group known as the New Edwardians. This had some relationship to developments in female dress. Interestingly, too, the 'teddy boy' as a style and term was to emerge within a couple of years.

The most significant trend in men's styles this year was the jettisoning of the matching waistcoat in favour of something in a complementary or contrasting colour. Such supplementary garments might use a variety of materials including corduroy, silk and velvet. Bolder designs and colours were also seen in shirts, socks and ties. The style of the double-breasted lounge suit jacket was 'button–two, show–three'. Both the collar and lapels would be fairly long. However, while sleeves often carried two-inch turn-back cuffs, the trousers had no turn-ups, and might be quite narrow. The corduroy jacket – sometimes of surprising colours (sea-green, for instance) – was much in vogue. With side vents and jetted pockets, it would be worn with worsted trousers with deep turn-ups. Crepe-soled suede shoes and a lightweight cap or hat matching the colour of the jacket completed the look for the man of fashion.

The Duke of Edinburgh made quite an impact when he wore a 1952 version of the Norfolk jacket with full-cut plus-fours. The jacket had two large pouch cross-pockets and two outside vertical pockets. Sleeves were close-fitting at the wrists with strap and button fastening. The three-quarter-length socks were woven in a wide rib.

OFF THE PEG

Formal clothes were much the same as those which had been worn in the 1930s and 1940s. Older men's informal clothes were still traditional too. Even on holiday, trousers, sports jacket, collar and tie would normally be worn. But those in their late twenties or early thirties began to leave off waistcoats or pullovers, revealing white shirts and red braces. But the jacket would remain firmly on and the hat was still quite popular, though not as universally as it had been before the war. Overall, a census of that year showed 56.7 per cent wore some

form of headwear. 'Bowler Hat Week' had been launched in 1950 to celebrate a hundred years of wearing that item. Although not a major success, it meant that the hat was still a standard – perhaps expected – feature of the well-dressed businessman in 1952. The trilby, in brown and grey, was the most popular style for informal wear. Rebel/arty fashion for the young middle class meant the oversize sweater and (black) polo-neck jumper. The anorak, parka and 'lumber' jacket together with the long, open-ended zips were still a few years away.

Young boys still wore short trousers and school blazers over shirts and ties. Pullovers, a much-favoured Christmas present, often replaced jackets indoors. Socks were always to the knee. But on holiday things changed, with short-sleeved shirts (for girls as well as boys) and sandals worn without socks.

HAIR AND COSMETICS

While it was still usual to wash and style hair at home, home permanent-waving chemical solutions could be dangerous and uncertain. Consequently more women began to use professional hairdressers. Typically the hair would be cut and permed every six or seven weeks. Depending on the money available, some would go to the hairdresser once a fortnight or even once a week to have it washed and set. Even schoolgirls slept in wire and coin rollers, kept in place by hairnets or scarves. One thirteen-year-old girl asked at school to complete the phrase 'uneasy lies the head . . .' answered '. . . that wears curlers in bed at night'. The teacher was not amused and she had to write out the correct response ('that wears the crown') several times!

Boys and men normally went to the barbers about once a month for a 'short back and sides'. Long hair was considered decadent and resonant with 'unmanliness'. Girls often pushed shoulder-length hair under a band.

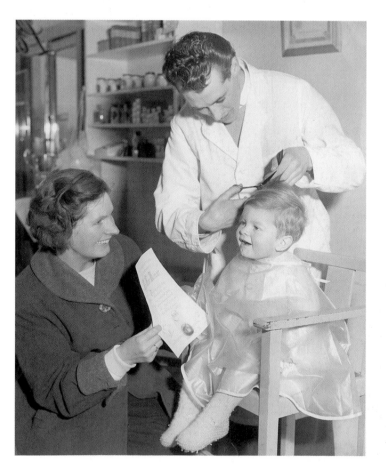

This little boy is having his first haircut. His mother is showing him his certificate which has one of his baby curls attached.

SEVEN

The Arts, the Pictures and the Church

THE NATION AND THE ARTS

John Ruskin argued that 'war is the foundation of all the arts'. Certainly the experience, nature and outcome of the Second World War had made a significant impact on those who created the arts and those who wished to experience them. At the same time it also witnessed an increased role in the arts for government both during the conflict and subsequently. The developments of the postwar period included the foundation of the Arts Council of Great Britain, set up in 1946, and the National Film Finance Corporation which was formed three years later. The Arts Council emerged from the wartime Committee for the Encouragement of Music and the Arts. Its aim was to provide 'the Best for the Most'. The British Council was made responsible for promoting British arts

BOOKS OF THE YEAR

Hemlock and After,
  Angus Wilson
Lieutenant Hornblower,
  C.S. Forrester
Doting, Henry Green
Men at Arms, Evelyn Waugh
Mr Nicholas, Thomas Hinde
A Buyer's Market,
  Anthony Powell
Excellent Women,
  Barbara Pym
The Struggles of Albert Woods,
  William Cooper
Prisoner of Grace, Joyce Cary

Evelyn Waugh with his wife Laura.

overseas. Annual festivals were established at Cheltenham (1945), Edinburgh (1947), Bath (1948) and Aldeburgh (1948). Both the institutions and the festivals listed above were active in 1952.

LITERATURE

One of the moods generated in the aftermath of the Second World War was that of disillusion with the official patriotic and heroic myth. The first part of Evelyn Waugh's trilogy reflecting this outlook appeared in 1952. *Men at Arms* opens at the outbreak of war when Guy Crouchback, the leading protagonist in the trilogy, is thirty-five and living quietly in Italy. He returns to England, enlists in the Halberdiers and has a somewhat inglorious military career.

The political outlook of the first postwar generation was more sceptical, even cynical, than that of most of their predecessors of the 1930s. *Hemlock and After*, Angus Wilson's first novel, was a satire whose underlying theme is the inadequacy of liberalism. His characters are 'expertly portrayed and uniformly unendearing', in the words of one contemporary critic. Thomas Hinde's *Mr Nicholas* was also a first novel. At the time this was seen as a devastating analysis of English upper-middle-class family life in the Surrey stockbroker belt. C.P. Snow described it as 'one of the best novels of the year'. *Doting* was Henry Green's last novel. In it he observed without sympathy the vagaries of middle-aged passion.

On a lighter note this year also saw C.S. Forester's *Lieutenant Hornblower* and Anthony Powell's *A Buyer's Market* (the second part in the novel sequence 'A Dance to the Music of Time') as well as works by Barbara Pym (*Excellent Women*), William Cooper (*The Struggles of Albert Woods*) and Joyce Cary (*Prisoner of Grace*).

In terms of poetry, the year saw the collected shorter poems of Ezra Pound and the collected poems of the Scottish poet Edwin Muir. Although Muir ignored the trends in modern poetry, he was much admired by T.S. Eliot, who wrote the preface for a later, definitive version. Dylan Thomas's *Collected Poems 1934–1952* was also published this year. He was to die in 1953.

John O'CONNOR   *RIP 1952*

A Roman Catholic who was ordained in 1895 at the age of twenty-five, he was for many years the parish priest of St Cuthbert's, Bradford. In 1904 he met G.K. Chesterton, whom he received into the Catholic Church in 1922. Chesterton based his characterisation of the priest-detective Father Brown on Mgr O'Connor. O'Connor in turn wrote *Father Brown on Chesterton* in 1938.

THEATRE

There was no British National Theatre in 1952 but its foundation stone had been laid in July 1951. Equally, no new theatre was built at this time but several which had been damaged during the war were repaired or converted for other uses. The Shakespeare Memorial Theatre had a reasonable year, as did the Old Vic in London. Altogether there were some fifty theatres in London, and the Open Air Theatre in Regent's Park was also operational. Some actors trained with the Royal Academy of Dramatic Art, others at the Old Vic in Bristol. But for many their first experience of taking to the boards was through one of the 33,000 amateur dramatic societies that were then active in Britain.

In terms of theatre entertainment, 1952 will perhaps be best remembered for the opening of *The Mousetrap* by Agatha Christie. It was based on a short radio play entitled *Three Blind Mice* and it was the author's son-in-law who came up with the new title (there was already another play under the original title) and her grandson Matthew who was to benefit from *The Mousetrap*'s profits. Originally starring Richard Attenborough and his wife Sheila Sim, the play was expected to run for about eight months – but it was still being performed fifty years later! Frederick Knott's *Dial M for Murder* was also in performance at this time.

Another of the year's successes was *The Young Elizabeth* by Jeannette Dowling and Francis Letton which opened in April. Starring May Morris, it dealt with the girlhood of Queen Elizabeth I and, after the period of Court mourning was over, it was the first

The original cast of *The Mousetrap*, which opened on 25 November 1952. Third from the left is Richard Attenborough and third from the right is Sheila Sim.

play to be seen by Queen Elizabeth II. Meanwhile Margaret Johnson was to prove a great success in both Tennessee Williams' *Summer and Smoke* and Philip Barry's *Second Threshold* (which also featured Clive Brook). There was also Noel Coward's *Quadrille* with Alfred Lunt and Lynn Fontanne, and *Winter Journey* by Clifford Odets, in which a broken-down actor was played by Michael Redgrave, his director by Sam Wanamaker (an American actor new to London who would later re-establish The Globe theatre) and his wife by Googie Withers. Henry James's works were to inspire *Letter from Paris* and *The Innocents* (based on *The Turn of the Screw*) with Flora Robson. Katharine Hepburn ensured the success of Bernard Shaw's *The Millionairess*. The American musicals *Call Me Madam* and *Porgy and Bess* were also well received. *South Pacific* continued to be successful in both London and New York.

Among contemporary British dramatists whose work was performed in 1952 were Terence Rattigan (*The Deep Blue Sea*), J.B. Priestley (*The Dragon's Mouth*) and Christopher Fry (*The First Born*). The Rattigan play was the story of a judge's wife's unrequited love for a young pilot, which caused her to contemplate suicide. It starred Peggy Ashcroft (and subsequently Celia Johnson) as the wife, Roland Culver as the judge and Kenneth More as the pilot. The BBC Home Service also promoted twentieth-century drama in its series *The English Theatre*.

As far as Shakespeare was concerned, the year saw, among others, John Gielgud's production of *Much Ado About Nothing* and *Romeo and Juliet* (with Alan Badel and Claire Bloom as the lovers). There was also Thomas Middleton's *A Trick to Catch the Old One*, which was produced on the Elizabethan stage of Bernard Miles's private theatre, The Mermaid.

AT THE THEATRE

The Mousetrap,
  Agatha Christie
The Young Elizabeth,
  Jeanette Dowling and
  Francis Lenton
Quadrille, Noel Coward
Winter Journey,
  Clifford Odets
The Deep Blue Sea,
  Terence Rattigan
The Dragon's Mouth,
  J.B. Priestley
The First Born,
  Christopher Fry

Gertrude LAWRENCE   *RIP 1952*

Born in London in 1898, this celebrated British actress was educated at the Convent of the Sacred Heart, Streatham. She first appeared on stage in 1910 at the Brixton Theatre, London, as a child dancer in *Babes in the Wood*. Working in the provinces for a while, she enjoyed her first stage success in 1916 with *Some*. Within a few years she was nationally known for her singing, dancing, acting and lively personality. She went to the USA in the early 1920s and became such good friends with Noel Coward that he wrote *Private Lives* (1930) especially for her. She toured with him in 1935 with *Tonight at 7.30*. Her best-known later performances were as Susan Trexel in *Susan and God* (New York, 1937) and as Lydia Kenyon in *Skylark* (New York, 1939). In London she was best remembered for the role of Stella Martyn in Daphne du Maurier's *September Tide* (1948). At the time of her death she was playing Anna in *The King and I* in New York.

MUSIC

There were seasons of opera and ballet in London at the Royal Opera House, Covent Garden, at Sadler's Wells and at Glyndebourne. Other companies active at this time included the Carl Rosa (one of the oldest opera organisations in Britain) and the English Opera Group, which had been formed in 1947.

Interest in modern opera was growing, as demonstrated for example by Paul Hindemith's *Mathis der Maler* (*Mathis the Painter*) which was well received at the 1952 Edinburgh International Festival of Music and Drama (its full name). More traditional fare was on offer at the Glyndebourne Festival with works by Mozart (*Idomeneo* and *Cosi fan tutte*), Rossini and Verdi. The conductors were Vittorio Gui and John Pritchard. At the Aldeburgh Festival Benjamin Britten's *Love in a Village* was performed with an orchestra of twelve. Highlights of the Cheltenham Festival included the Hallé Orchestra under Sir John Barbirolli and the City of Birmingham Orchestra under Rudolf Schwarz. New works featured there included a symphony for strings by William Wordsworth (a descendant of the poet), which was receiving its first performance after fifteen years, and a string quartet by Richard Arnell. Vaughan Williams completed *Symphonia Antarctica*, a development of the music he had written for the film *Scott of the Antarctic* (1949). It did not receive its first performance, however, until 1953.

Ralph Vaughan Williams.

In September and October Arturo Toscanini conducted the Philharmonia Orchestra of London in two concerts at the Festival Hall. He performed Brahms' four symphonies. This was Toscanini's first appearance in Britain since 1939. The year witnessed the first English performances of, among other works, Arthur Benjamin's *Piano Concerto*, Sir Arthur Bliss's *The Enchantress* (sung by Kathleen Ferrier; she died the following year) and Peter Racine Fricker's *Second Symphony*.

The BBC Henry Wood Promenade Concerts (the 'Proms') continued to be popular, although there were criticisms over the continued absence of lesser known works by famous composers and the failure to play the symphonies of such modern British composers as Britten, Bush, Moeran and Tippett. Malcolm Sargent (who himself had been a composer-conductor at the Proms over thirty years earlier) came to the defence of the Proms and its audiences (which averaged 5,000 with twenty-four sell-out nights). Even so, there were no premieres or first English performances. That said, there were several works which had not previously been performed at a promenade concert. These included works by Britten and Fricker. Larry Adler played the *Romance for Harmonica* with strings and piano by Vaughan Williams. The popularity of the work was such that the audience demanded (and secured) an immediate repeat. It also did much to raise the status of the mouth organ. This was the last year of the Winter Proms until the 1970s, as falling support meant that they were no longer viable.

Also performed in London (but not at the Proms) at this time was Edith Sitwell's poem 'The Shadow of Cain', accompanied by music in the twelve-note idiom by Humphrey Searle. Written in 1946, the poem was Sitwell's response to the horror of the atomic bombing of Hiroshima. The work had a mixed reception.

The season of BBC symphony concerts began in mid-October by celebrating Ralph Vaughan Williams' eightieth birthday. The Third Programme also broadcast a complete cycle of *Der Ring* with *Parsifal* and *Die Meistersinger* from Bayreuth and the first world performance of Richard Strauss's *Die Liebe der Danae*. At least one full-length opera was broadcast each week. One particularly significant work was the Covent Garden presentation of Alban Berg's *Wozzeck*. There was also an extensive study of Arnold Schoenberg, which included concerts.

CONTEMPORARY ARTISTS

Among the leading figures in the world of British art at this time were Stanley Spencer, Graham Sutherland, John Piper and Ben Nicholson. A new generation, however, was beginning to emerge, as witnessed by the work of Francis Bacon, Lucian Freud and John Bratby, who was the best known member of the early 1950s Kitchen Sink School (a term coined by art critic David Sylvester in 1954). The group sought to portray the harsh nature of contemporary life through realistic representations of dustbins, milk bottles, beer bottles and the debris of ordinary domestic existence. Although

David Bomberg belonged to the older generation, he was in the process of shaping the next. Between 1945 and 1953 Bomberg taught part-time at the Borough Polytechnic (subsequently the South Bank University, London). Frank Auerbach and Leon Kossof were among his pupils at this time. The major names in sculpture were Henry Moore and Barbara Hepworth, while those in the process of becoming established at this time were Lynn Chadwick, Reg Butler and Kenneth Armitage, who first exhibited in 1952.

Chadwick had trained as an architect and had only taken up sculpture after serving as a pilot in the Second World War. 'Balanced sculptures' perhaps best describes his output at this time as, like Giacometti, British sculptors generally chose to work through modelling or welding rather than carving. His *Inner Eye* (Maquette III) was created in 1952. It comprises a piece of rough crystal precariously held in balance within a cage-like iron structure. Reg Butler was another architect turned sculptor. In a series of iron sculptures Butler reduced the human figure to a taut arrangement of linear abstract forms. In 1952 he submitted an open construction to the international competition for a monument to the Unknown Political Prisoner. He won the prize, even though he was up against people like Gabo and Hepworth. Butler's original preliminary model or maquette was enlarged into a working model but Cold War politics meant that the actual monument was never developed further. It was to have been over 300 feet high and Butler intended the construction to allude symbolically to the various ways in which people had suffered for their beliefs – the cage, cross, guillotine, scaffold and watch tower would all have featured.

ART INSTITUTIONS AND EXHIBITIONS

The President of the Royal Academy in 1952 was Sir Gerald Kelly, who had succeeded Sir Alfred Munnings in 1949. He was a celebrated portrait painter who oversaw some very successful exhibitions during his presidency – staged partly to boost the Academy's deteriorating finances. In 1952 these included the Leonardo da Vinci Quincentenary, which covered the full range of that artist's genius, primarily through drawings. It was probably the finest such exhibition to date with loans from the Royal Collection at Windsor and the British Museum. Although no masterpiece paintings were included there was, for instance, a series of sketches for such works as *The Last Supper*.

The exhibition also included scientific working models, constructed from his drawings by the Science Museum, and a section dealing with da Vinci's literary interests. Such was its popularity that it was extended until September and was seen by some 200,000 people. It was followed by an exhibition of the work of Sir Frank Brangwyn. This was the first time that the Academy had held a retrospective display of the work of a living member.

Among the art on display at the Summer Exhibition which opened in May was work by Winston Churchill. He had been made the first Honorary Academician Extraordinary in 1948 and had had his paintings shown for the first time at the previous year's Summer Exhibition when he had sent in work, unknown to the Selection Committee, under the pseudonym David Winter. Thereafter his paintings featured in every Summer Exhibition until his death in 1965. About 150,000 came to the exhibition in 1952: one of the paintings to attract considerable attention was *The Revolt in the Desert* by William Roberts. The Winter Exhibition consisted of Dutch Masters. Though a small group of important paintings was on loan from the Netherlands, most came from English collections and over forty Rembrandts were on display.

There were exhibitions at the Tate on the work of Gwen John and Jacob Epstein while John Constable, Roger Fry and Max Beerbohm were honoured elsewhere in the capital. Beerbohm had been a friend of Oscar Wilde, who once described him as someone who enjoyed 'the gift of perpetual old age'. Now in his eightieth year he was certainly enjoying celebrity status in the art and literary world.

CINEMA

The state was actively involved in supporting the British film industry. A quota system operated whereby British output was to occupy 30 per cent of screen time for long films and 25 per cent for short. Three groups originated by the National Film Finance Corporation (British Film Makers Ltd at Pinewood, the Elstree Group and Group Three) together with London Films and Ealing Studios produced most British feature films. British documentary work was almost ended by the Conservative government when the Crown Film Unit and the Mobile Film Exhibition Units both ceased to function at the end of March.

The chief British feature film productions of the year included *The Sound Barrier* and *The Importance of Being Earnest*. The former, directed by David Lean, was a topical story about an aircraft manufacturer's attempt to break the sound barrier. Written by Terence Rattigan, it starred Ralph Richardson, Nigel Patrick, Ann Todd and Dinah Sheridan. It secured three BAFTA awards and Terence Rattigan was nominated for an Oscar. Anthony Asquith's version of Wilde's play had a mixed reception but Edith Evans's role as Lady Bracknell, although not necessarily definitive, continues to overshadow all others who play the part – especially when it comes to uttering the words 'A handbag!' The other actors in the film were Michael Redgrave, Dorothy Tutin and Joan Greenwood.

Other films which appeared in 1952 were *Cry the Beloved Country* and *Outcast of the Islands*. The former was based on the novel by Alan Paton and directed by Zoltan Korda. It starred Sidney Poitier, Joyce Carey and Geoffrey Keen and was structured around the contrasting lives of a rich white farmer and a black preacher living in poverty in a shanty town. It was filmed in Johannesburg and, like the novel, adopted a sympathetic view towards the victims of South Africa's racial policies. *Outcast of the Islands* was directed by Carol Reed and based on a Joseph Conrad novel about a man in the tropics

Vera Lynn, a huge star of the period. She had three songs in the first British music chart in 1952.

Al Martino.

who drifts and ultimately sinks to his own destruction. It starred Trevor Howard, Ralph Richardson and Robert Morley.

In a rather different vein was *Mandy*. Directed by Alexander Mackendrick, it starred Jack Hawkins, Phyllis Calvert and Mandy Miller (who played the title role). It told the story of a little girl, born deaf, who was sent to a special school and learnt how to speak. Jack Hawkins, who was subsequently to lose his voice in real life, played the head of the deaf and dumb school. It was shot in such a school in Manchester. Jack Hawkins also starred in probably the most commercially successful film of the year, *Angels One Five*, in which he played a group captain in a fighter station during the Battle of Britain. His success led to his being offered many service roles thereafter. Mandy Miller is probably now best remembered for her recording of the children's favourite 'Nellie the Elephant'. Among the American films which cinema-goers saw this year were *The Snows of Kilimanjaro*, *The Greatest Show on Earth*, *High Noon*, *Limelight*, *Moulin Rouge* and *Singin' in the Rain*.

POPULAR MUSIC

The first British music chart as featured in the *New Musical Express*, 14 November 1952

Here in My Heart Al Martino
You Belong to Me Jo Stafford
Feet Up Guy Mitchell
Because You're Mine
   Mario Lanza
Isle of Innisfree Bing Crosby
Half as Much
   Rosemary Clooney
Somewhere Along the Way
   Nat King Cole
High Noon Frankie Laine
Forget Me Not Vera Lynn
Sugarbush Doris Day &
   Frankie Laine
Blue Tango Ray Martin
Homing Waltz Vera Lynn
Auf Wiederseh'n Vera Lynn

A distinctive youth culture was more evident in the mid- than the early 1950s, with the coming of rock 'n' roll (a term originally coined in the 1930s) through the records and films of first Bill Haley and then Elvis Presley. But from the start of the decade, the market for commercial popular music was increasingly a teenage one. Popular music had traditionally been written for the family, not primarily for youth. *New Musical Express*, launched in 1952, helped to bring about this change as it almost immediately aimed for a teenage readership. It was this paper that first published the English hit parade. Al Martino's 'Here in my Heart' topped the *New Musical Express*'s first official singles chart on 15 November 1952. Vera Lynn's 'Auf Wiederseh'n, Sweetheart' was a particularly popular record in both Britain and the USA. It was the first-ever British record to top the hit parade simultaneously on both sides of the Atlantic.

THE BBC

In 1952 the BBC's charter was renewed for a further ten years but there were changes – some of which were controversial. The Corporation was to continue as the sole provider of radio but others might provide an additional television service. This was a policy favoured by the Conservative government and was widely presumed at the time to pave the way for commercial television, which did indeed start operating in 1955. The Director General of the BBC, Sir

William Haley, resigned on 30 September. He had held the post since 1944 and left to become editor of *The Times*. His successor was Sir Ian Jacob.

In recognition of the work of the Corporation's first Director General, the Reith Lectures had been introduced in 1947. Professor Arnold Toynbee gave these lectures for 1952. His subject was 'The World and the West'. The word order within the title was deliberate, as Professor Toynbee sought to explore how the majority of humanity viewed the West. The philosopher Bertrand Russell gave an impressive series under the title 'Portraits from Memory'. Those chosen included D.H. Lawrence, Sidney and Beatrice Webb, John Maynard Keynes and Lytton Strachey. Among those also appearing on the network were Isaiah Berlin and Thomas Mann.

Bertrand Russell.

In March 1952 there was a programme on the Home Service which discussed Britain's role in Europe. The participants were Paul Reynaud (French prime minister in 1940), Paul Henri Spaak (a former Belgian prime minister) and a Danish journalist. All urged British participation in the formation of what was already termed Federal Europe with, according to Spaak, the creation of a European army and a constitution for Europe being the main challenges for the current year. Sir Anthony Eden, the Foreign Secretary, in a separate broadcast, said that the UK could not join any such federation because the nation's vision was beyond Europe. He spoke of Britain being on the fringe of three interlocking worlds. In addition to Europe there were the Commonwealth ('a strong and subtle factor in world stability') and the North Atlantic Association. He wished both the unification of the European steel and coal industry (the Schuman Plan) and the formation of a European army success.

THE CHRISTIAN CHURCH

Christianity continued to be an important feature in people's lives in 1952 – the Church of England in particular. The sovereign was required by law to be a member of the Anglican church and was ultimately responsible for the appointment of archbishops, bishops and deans. Elizabeth II's first appointment was Michael Ramsey. He was made Bishop of Durham and went on to become Archbishop of Canterbury. But at the start of 1952 he was Regius Professor of Divinity at Cambridge and Durham was to be his first see. On being asked whether it was uncomfortable to wear the garments required of a bishop, he replied 'They are like false teeth. At first they irritate a bit but when you are used to them you find them serviceable.'

The first half of the twentieth century had seen short periods of decline and growth in the number of churchgoers successively in

Michael Ramsey, Bishop of Durham.

each decade. Probably just under one in five of the population attended a place of worship weekly, though fewer now went twice on Sunday than in the past. But Christianity's influence was wider than its active membership implied. Church schools provided day school education and since the 1944 ('Butler') Education Act, Catholic school provision in particular was increasing. There were twenty-two Anglican theological colleges and twenty-four Anglican colleges for training teachers.

There were also Sunday Schools which were attended by a sizeable minority of children, possibly up to the age of fifteen (when most left day school too). Equally, people retained a strong attachment to Christian baptisms, marriages and funerals. Probably about a third of all males were confirmed into the Anglican church, and even more females. The service for the thanksgiving (or 'churching') of women after childbirth continued to be requested. Even so the importance of home mission was recognised and new methods of evangelising deployed. In one town teams of clergy visited public houses where they sat as a brains trust to answer questions from the regulars. The first British worker-priests began in 1952 – as miners in the Kent coalfield. There were also factory and industrial chaplains.

However, inadequate funding was already something of a problem for the Anglican church and measures such as the merging of parishes were taken. None the less work had resumed on the construction of Guildford Cathedral. The foundation stone (from Jarrow) had been laid in July 1936 but building work stopped with the outbreak of war. An appeal was launched in 1952 for £86,000 to complete it.

The leading Nonconformist churches were the Methodists, Congregationalists and Baptists. Only the latter two had admitted women to the Ministry by 1952, although both the Methodists and Anglicans were to do so before the century was out. Deaconesses were not considered at this time to hold Holy Orders. The British Catholic community, headed by Cardinal Griffin, was growing rapidly at this time: the number of priests, conversions and marriages were all increasing. In all, there were almost four million adherents and nearly two thousand parishes. Non-Catholics were required to convert to be married in the Catholic church and the mass was said in Latin.

Dr Fisher, Archbishop of Canterbury.

SUNDAY UNDER THREAT

Sunday was clearly different from the other days of the week and remained special to most Christians. In an age when many people were still working for part of Saturday, it was the only complete day of rest (for many men at least!) and what could be done on that day was limited by local or national laws, affecting in particular public house licensing hours, trading and entertainment. Only corner shops (as opposed to chain stores) could open that day and there were limits on what could be sold. It was illegal, for instance, to sell Bibles, and public houses were closed all day in some ('dry') areas of Wales. Sunday was known to many people as the Lord's Day and the Lord's Day Observance Society championed the way they believed He wanted it to be spent.

Despite a large if somewhat complex body of law (partly dating back to the fifteenth century), the Society noted in 1952 that there was 'widespread disregard for God's Commandment' (to rest on the Sabbath Day). Even so the Society's journals for that year could record many successes by members and others to prevent the arrival of what was sometimes termed 'the continental Sunday' or the 'pollution' of that day. Bideford Art Gallery had been prevented from opening on Sundays and a change of day secured for a motor-cycle scramble at Cheltenham. In July, however, six MPs (three from each of the main political parties) tabled a motion asking for a Select Committee to examine the law relating to Sunday entertainment with a view to ensuring that it was 'in accord with the present-day majority beliefs'. One of the MPs in an interview said he did not see 'why theatres, cinemas, shops, football and sport generally should not be available if people want them'. Furthermore, in the evening of Sunday 6 July the BBC Light Programme launched *Sports Review*. This was justified to the Society as being a response to public demand. Yet, noted the Society, the Corporation was not so sympathetic to those who wanted scientists with a Christian outlook to reply to evolutionists.

CHRISTIANITY AND BROADCASTING

In an address to the British Council of Churches in 1948, Sir William Haley, Director General of the BBC, spoke on 'Moral Values in Broadcasting'. He said that 'We are citizens of a Christian country, and the BBC – an institution set up by the State – bases its policy upon a positive attitude towards the Christian values . . . It seeks to safeguard . . . and foster acceptance of them.' Consequently, as he remained in post for most of 1952, Christianity was still relatively important in the weekly (indeed daily) broadcasting schedule.

The BBC broadcast the *Daily Service* at 10.15. When introduced in 1928, this had begun the broadcasting day. Church services were also broadcast on some days of the week and prayers featured in

Children's Hour as well as during the *Sunday Half Hour* which was mainly community hymn singing. There were religious discussions and, dating back to the start of the Corporation itself, the *Epilogue*. But services had yet to be broadcast during normal church hours.

The BBC limited religious broadcasts to those bodies 'within the main stream of historic Christianity'. This policy excluded, among others, Christian Scientists, Christian Spiritualists, Swedenborgians and Unitarians. No Jewish or Muslim services had ever been broadcast, although there were Jewish talks on the eve of that faith's major festivals.

Until the eve of 1952, television had played only a minor part in religious broadcasting. But transmissions in December 1951 included carol singing from Westminster Abbey and Trafalgar Square, services from St Paul's Cathedral and Wesley's Chapel, City Road, London, and a meditation before the crib. Discussion was already under way that year over whether to televise communion and christening services. The broadcasting of the coronation service in 1953 (which included Holy Communion) led to more sacramental broadcasting thereafter.

JEWS AND MOSLEMS

In the wake of the horrors Jews faced on the continent during the Second World War, the British Jewish community was now the largest in Europe. During 1952 the Chief Rabbi of the British Empire, Israel Brodie, carried out a pastoral tour to Jewish communities in Australia and New Zealand. The head office of the World Sephardic Federation was transferred at this time from Paris to London and a rabbinical college and teachers' training seminary were established at Ramsgate for the Sephardic community.

The British Muslim community grew in the wake of postwar migration. Its principal mosque was at Woking but mosques had already been established in London, Birmingham, Manchester, Cardiff and Glasgow.

The Sporting Year

CRICKET

Surrey, led by Surridge, won the County Championship by 256 points, the highest to date for the scoring system deployed. Yorkshire and Lancashire were runners-up, with Derbyshire and Leicestershire performing well. The Gentlemen v. Players game produced a splendid finish – the Players won by two runs in the last over of the day. Leading by 119 runs on the first innings, the Gentlemen were set 322 to win. They started poorly but 127 runs by C.H. Palmer, aided by courageous hitting by F.R. Brown and D.J. Insole, almost gave them victory.

In the University match Cambridge could field their test match players David Sheppard, Peter May, John Warr and the South African Cuan McCarthy; Oxford had only one player of equal class – (Michael) Colin Cowdrey, whose initials correctly anticipated his enthusiastic father's hopes for his son's cricket career. (Indeed, even at this stage Cowdrey had already made cricketing history, having been the youngest player ever to appear in a public schools match at Lord's – at the age of thirteen.) Oxford achieved a first innings total of 272 runs. Sheppard declared at 408 for 8 before lunch on the last day. Oxford was soon 94 for 6 but managed to hold out for a draw.

The first England test match since the war was held in 1946. It was against India, captained by Wally Hammond and held at Lord's. It was also televised and Brian Johnston was the commentator. Not until the opening of the Sutton Coldfield transmitter, however, was the BBC able to broadcast live from outside London. This happened in 1950 when matches from Trent Bridge could be shown. But it was only in 1952, with the opening of the Holme Moss transmitter, that those from Headingley and Old Trafford could also feature.

It was this year too that for the first time a professional – Len Hutton – was appointed as captain of England in England (James Lillywhite, Alfred Shaw and Arthur Shrewsbury had captained England in Australia while Jack Hobbs had taken over the captaincy for two days at Old Trafford when Arthur Carr had been taken ill

Fred Truman runs into the pavilion at Old Trafford after taking 8 Indian wickets for 31 runs, August 1952. 'The only time to worry is when you lose', he said.

with tonsillitis). This caused considerable controversy because it was felt that only an amateur truly understood the demands of the game and the needs of the players. But no harm was done, the precedent had been created and was repeated. Hutton led England to victory in three matches against India (the fourth was drawn).

Another first for test cricket in 1952 was the inclusion of Fred Truman in the side which played against India (led by Vijay Hazare). A true heavyweight at the very start of his life (at birth he weighed just over 14 pounds) as well as at the start of his test match career at the age of twenty-one, he gave his first England cap to his mother. When India batted for a second time at Headingley, they were only 41 runs behind England. But they lost their first four wickets for no runs in the first fourteen balls – Truman bowled out three in eight balls, Bedser got the other. This score – 0 for 4 – was the worst ever start by a Test side. In all, Truman took seven wickets in this match, eight at Lord's, nine at Old Trafford and five at the only innings at The Oval. Truman bowled fast and with far more accuracy at Old Trafford than at Lord's. His first innings figures – 8 for 31 in 8.4 overs – were some of the most remarkable in test history. In the second innings, Bedser and Laker were also very accurate.

Significant achievements of the season included Godfrey Evans securing a first at the second test at Lord's: no previous England wicket-keeper had made a hundred dismissals in tests. Similarly not for some time had two amateurs – Sheppard and May – headed the first-class batting averages. They and Hutton each averaged over 60 for more than 2,000 runs apiece. By the end of the 1952 season, taking his career as a whole to date, Hutton had scored 34,205 runs for an average of 50.16, had represented England sixty times and scored 114 centuries. Truman had the best bowling figures (61 wickets for 841 runs), followed by Bedser (154 for 2530). Wardle of Yorkshire took most wickets – 177.

An enduring memory of the 1952 test matches for Brian Johnston, however, was a conversation with the Indian manager who understandably spoke highly of his team. Johnston asked him whether he was a selector. 'No' he replied, 'I'm a Christian!'

FOOTBALL

The highest seasonal aggregate attendance in the Football League was in 1948/9 when there were over forty-one million spectators. Attendances thereafter began to show a steady decline. The 1951/2 season totalled just over thirty-nine million, down by 1.5 per cent on the previous year, most of which was the result of lower gates at First Division matches. The numbers attending actually increased in the Second Division and Third Division North. The highest single day saw 1,085,764 spectators at football matches; the lowest recorded figure for the season was 526,201.

The overall decline in numbers was attributed to many things, especially increased live coverage of games. Radio commentaries of football matches had begun as early as January 1927 and since 1938 all Cup Finals had been broadcast live. This policy, together with showing internationals, was resumed when television returned after the war. But whereas there were only 10,000–12,000 viewers in the late 1930s, by 1950 some 386,750 sets had been licensed, representing a potential audience of over a million.

There were changes in the divisions in this season. Huddersfield Town (which had never before been relegated) and Fulham lost their places in the First Division to Sheffield Wednesday and Cardiff City. Coventry City and Queen's Park Rangers were relegated from the Second to the Third Division, being replaced by Plymouth Argyle (South) and Lincoln City (North). At the Football League's Annual Meeting for 1952 the non-league clubs Darlington, Workington, Exeter and Walsall were re-elected. New Brighton's application was not supported: on learning of this the club then asked the league for help to pay off debts of £2,800.

This was still the era of the maximum wage for footballers, which was £14 per week while playing and £10 per week during the close season; £30 was paid for an international match. The number of players on the maximum wage increased significantly, from 255 to 730. Some players were able to supplement this by other means. For instance, Stanley Matthews was paid £20 a week for endorsing Co-operative Wholesale Society football boots. Admission prices also increased. In 1952 the minimum ticket price for a football match, including entertainment tax, was 1s 9d.

There was also the issue of transfer fees. In March 1952 the findings of the Forster Committee (whose members included the cricketer Herbert Sutcliffe) were published as a White Paper. The committee thought that the ideal system for the transfer of players was a straight swap between clubs but recognised that, as a general way of operating, this was impracticable. It recommended instead that there should be a maximum transfer fee of £15,000. The sum received should be divided equally between the Football Association, the Professional Footballers' Benevolent Fund and the transferring club.

The first official match under floodlighting since 1878 took place in the 1951/2 season. It took place at Highbury on 19 September 1951 when Arsenal entertained the Hapoel club of Tel Aviv in a friendly. Some 44,000 watched the Gunners win an easy victory (6–1). Several years earlier Herbert Chapman, manager of Arsenal between 1926 and 1934, had had floodlighting built into the West Stand but the Football Association had banned its use in official matches at that time, fearing success would result in clubs 'spending too much money'. Another technology which as far as football was concerned still lay in the future was flight. Teams normally travelled between grounds by rail. The league had withheld permission in 1932 for teams to fly because their insurance did not cover it. This restriction was only relaxed in 1957.

THE FA CUP

In the semi-finals Blackburn Rovers, a Second Division side, lost 1–2 to Newcastle and Chelsea 0–3 to Arsenal. Both matches were replayed after draws. Blackburn equalled Aston Villa's record of reaching the semi-finals fourteen times; the two clubs still held the record of six wins in the final. Walthamstow Avenue beat Leyton in the FA Amateur Cup Final.

On 3 May 1952 some 100,000 people (total gate money £39,351) watched Newcastle United become the first club to retain the FA Cup since Blackburn Rovers' two wins in 1890 and 1891. It was regarded as a very lucky win. In the 22nd minute of the game Arsenal's Wally Barnes, an international back, injured his knee. For a few minutes he played on with his leg strapped but then split a cartilage in a tackle on George Robledo. Also injured in this match were the Arsenal players Ray Daniel with his broken wrist in a cast, Lishman

Arsenal supporters at the front of the huge crowd at Wembley for the cup final, 3 May 1952. Newcastle were the winners, 1–0.

with a septic cut and Jimmy Logic with an internal haemorrhage. But Arsenal, under the captaincy of 38-year-old Joe Mercer, continued to defend brilliantly. Indeed, they almost took the lead 10 minutes from the end when a header by Lishman from Cox's corner bounced along the Newcastle crossbar. Extra time looked inevitable when, with only 6 minutes to go, Robledo scored the only goal of the match as the ball bounced in off a post. Winston Churchill presented the cup medals.

Joe Harvey, Newcastle's captain, believed that 'Joe Mercer is the greatest player I have ever met in this game'. Mercer incidentally had also been Harvey's former wartime sergeant-major. Stan Seymour, Newcastle's director-manager, paid this tribute to Arsenal: 'We won the Cup, but the glory is yours.' This sentiment was echoed by Tom Whitaker, the Arsenal manager, who declared, 'Boys, I have never been so proud of you in victory as I am in defeat.'

Manchester United had provided one of the biggest cup-tie surprises by losing 0–2 at home in their first game to Hull City, a Second Division team. But they won the Football League Championship by four points over the holders Tottenham Hotspur. Hibernian retained the Scottish League Division A title by four points over Rangers; Clyde headed Division B.

. . . AND FINALLY

In 1952 West Bromwich Albion received its Christmas present a day late. In the Boxing Day match at Hillsborough, three Sheffield Wednesday players, Vince Kenny, Norman Curtis and Eddie Gannon, scored own goals. West Bromwich went home with a 5–4 win.

GOLF

A major achievement that year was the first victory by a British team in the women's Curtis Cup match against the USA. Despite an impressive American entry for the women's championship at Troon, only one (Miss Murray) reached the semi-final. Two of the British Curtis Cup team fought out the longest final to date in the history of the championship. Miss Paterson eventually beat Miss Stephens at the 38th hole.

The South African Arthur Locke won the British Open Championship at Royal Lytham, Lancashire, finishing one stroke ahead of Peter Thomson of Australia. This was his third such victory in four years. Three British professionals – Weetman, Daly and Panton – each won two major tournaments, but the winner of the Verdon trophy was not decided until Weetman won the Masters. Among the new players beginning to make their mark was one Peter Alliss, who with Hunt won the two assistants' tournaments. Finally, in a challenge match at Walton Heath, Cotton (who first won the Open in 1934) with Daly easily defeated Locke and Browne to show that he remained one of the finest golfers in Britain at this time.

MOTOR-BOAT RACING

The outstanding event of 1952 was John Cobb's attempt at the world water speed record. In July Stanley Sayres' boat *Slo-Mo-Shun IV* had raised this to 178.49 mph. On 19 September Cobb's *Crusader* reached 173.14 mph on Loch Ness. Ten days later a second attempt was made, when he reached 240 mph. But before the end of the mile, the boat began to pitch and slow down. Immediately after completing the mile run, she bowed in and disintegrated. Cobb was flung out and killed. His speed over this single mile run was certified as 206.89 mph. He was thus the first person to travel at over 200 mph on water.

MOTOR RACING

The champion driver was Alberto Ascari driving a Ferrari. He won the fifth British Grand Prix held over a 250-mile course at Silverstone at 90.92 mph. Team-mate Taruffi was second while the British driver Mike Hawthorn was third in a Cooper-Bristol. The British Automobile Racing Club staged several international racing

John Cobb's jet-powered Crusader speedboat warming up on the shore of Loch Ness prior to the world water speed record.

John Rhodes COBB   *RIP 1952*

John Cobb was born in Esher, Surrey, in December 1899, and educated at Eton and Cambridge. A businessman whose first love was motor racing, he broke all the world records for time and distance up to 24 hours and held the lap record at 143.4 mph. In 1947 at Utah, and for the third time, he broke the world land speed record. This now stood at 394.2 mph but he reached 403 mph. He was killed while attempting the world water speed record on 29 September.

Stirling Moss on 30 January 1952 after coming second in the Monte Carlo Rally. He has just received his cup from Prince Rainier of Monaco.

meetings, including a nine-hour race involving night driving for the first time in Britain. It was won by Peter Collins and P.W.C. Griffith in a 2.5-litre Aston Martin, which covered 283 laps at an average speed of 75.42 mph.

In January Britain had its first success for twenty-one years in the Monte Carlo rally when the outright winner was Sidney Allard in a car built at his factory in South London. Allard was the only British competitor out of ninety-two entrants who finished the ride from Glasgow to Monaco without losing a mark. Stirling Moss (aged twenty-two) was second in a Sunbeam Talbot, only four points behind. There were five British cars in the first six places. The drivers faced harsh conditions of ice, snow and blizzards.

RUGBY UNION

The 1951/2 season was notable for the South African visit to Britain. The South Africans played thirty-one matches, losing only to the London Counties (9–11). They scored 562 points against 167. They were a particularly fit team, scoring 213:100 in the first halves and 349:67 after the intervals. The key members of the team included the half-backs du Toit and Brewis, the full-back Buchler and the wing three-quarter Ochse. The captain Kenyon was succeeded by Muller following an eye injury. South Africa beat Scotland 44–0; Wales by a try and a dropped goal to a try; England by a goal and a penalty goal to a try.

Wales won all four matches in the British home international championship and so won the Triple Crown for the ninth time. England beat Ireland by a try in a blizzard at Twickenham. Middlesex won the County Championship, beating Lancashire 9–6.

RUGBY LEAGUE

New Zealand visited Britain during the season, losing ten of its twenty-eight matches including all three tests. France retained the home international title on points average over Other Nationalities and England. Wales did not win a match. There was some anxiety over the quality of the Welsh players coming forward and this, plus the ban on recruiting Australian and New Zealand players, led to a suggestion that there should be a test series between Great Britain and France.

Wigan won the Northern Rugby League title for the fourth time since the war, beating Bradford Northern, which had finished top in ordinary games, by 13–6 in the final. In 1952 Workington Town was the first club outside Lancashire and Yorkshire to win the Challenge Cup, beating Featherstone 18–10 in the final at Wembley.

ROWING

The University Boat Race took place (and still does) between Putney and Mortlake, a distance of 4 miles, 1 furlong and 180 yards. In 1952 it took place on Saturday 29 March, which was the coldest late March day since records had begun at Kew in 1871. Under these circumstances several people recalled what had happened the previous year and wondered whether there might be a repeat. For in 1951, with Cambridge leading by some six lengths, the Oxford boat sank after hardly half a mile because of adverse weather and difficult rowing conditions. The race that year was abandoned in accordance with an agreement made in 1925 that if either crew had a serious accident before rowing a mile the race would be called off. It was re-run two days later and Cambridge won by twelve lengths in 20 minutes 50 seconds, its easiest win in fifty years.

In the 1952 race Cambridge won the toss and chose the Middlesex side. This was intended to provide the crew with shelter at the start of the race and enable it to establish a sufficient lead to cross over at Hammersmith and gain the advantage of the bend. Cambridge made a good start and soon led by about half a length. Oxford, however, drew level at Hammersmith Bridge and had the advantage of the bend. But the boats were still level at the Chiswick Steps. So close were the oars that on at least one occasion they seemed to touch.

The Oxford and Cambridge Boat Race, 1952. This was one of the closest-ever finishes to the event.

Oxford then increased the rate to 36/7 strokes per minute and secured victory in 20 minutes 23 seconds by a canvas (about 10 feet). It was Oxford's first victory since 1946 and its forty-fourth in the contest's history.

The first University Boat Race took place at Henley-on-Thames in 1829 and the interest this created subsequently encouraged the local townspeople to institute the Henley Regatta in 1839, making it the oldest rowing regatta in Europe. The following wind which blew throughout most of the four-day event in 1952 was, generally speaking, too strong for fast times. Even so several records were broken. The main event for the eights is the Grand Challenge Cup (1839). In the final of that event the Leander Club (Britain's Olympic eight) beat Sydney Rowing Club (the Australian Olympic crew) by half a length in 6 minutes 38 seconds. Another record was set by Radley College in winning the Princess Elizabeth Cup which was instituted in 1946 for school eights only.

TENNIS

Among those who attended the British hard court championships, played at the end of April at Bournemouth, were the men's singles title-holder Jaroslav Drobny, believed by many to be the world's finest player on hard courts, and Frank Sedgman of Australia, often regarded as the world's leading player on grass. The leading British players included Mottram, Paish, Horn and Becker. The Americans Doris Hart and Shirley Fry, champion and runner-up at Wimbledon in 1951 were also there. Drobny won the men's singles in a rain-soaked court; Doris Hart took the women's title.

On the Wimbledon courts in June the USA beat Great Britain 7–0 in the Wightman Cup. In the Wimbledon championships only two British players reached the last thirty-two of the men's singles. In the final Sedgman easily beat Drobny while in the final of the men's doubles McGregor and Sedgman enjoyed a comfortable victory over Seixas and Sturgess. Maureen Connolly, then aged seventeen, won the singles championship at her first attempt. She went on to win it again in 1953 and 1954. But partnered with Louise Brough for the women's doubles in 1952, she failed against Doris Hart and Shirley Fry.

HORSE RACING

There was little racing in early February as a result of frost and the king's death. Attendances were up, partly as a result of a cut in the entertainment tax which was reflected in lower admission prices.

Maureen Connolly, 'Little Mo', winner of the ladies' singles in 1952.

The two most important races at the National Hunt meeting at Cheltenham were both won by young French-bred geldings competing in the race for the first time. The Gold Cup was won by Miss D. Paget's Mont Tremblant, ridden by Dick and trained by Walwyn while the Champion Hurdle was won by Sir Ken. This horse was owned by Kingsley, trained by Stephenson and ridden by Molony.

The Aga Khan with his English-trained three-year-old colt Tulyar broke all British records for stake money won in a season. Tulyar, bred in Ireland by his owner, won all the seven races which he contested and showed himself to be the best horse in Europe. Among his successes were the Eclipse stakes, the St Leger and the King George VI and Queen Elizabeth stakes. The latter had been established in 1951 in connection with the Festival of Britain celebrations. It was the most valuable race in 1952, worth £23,302 10s.

The Derby was another of Tulyar's victories and he started the race as the 11–2 favourite. It was run on 28 May and was the richest to date

The Aga Khan watches the Jockey Club race at Chantilly, 15 June 1952.

Lester Piggott, riding one of the queen's horses, is led past the row of policemen by her majesty.

(£24,220 prize money) in the history of the race. It was the Aga Khan's fifth Derby win, equalling Lord Egremont's record set in the early nineteenth century. Gordon Richards initially led the field around Tattenham Corner on Monarch More but could not maintain the pace. Tulyar moved to take up the lead and finished three-quarters of a length ahead of Mrs Rank's Gay Time and Dupre's Faubourg II. Gay Time, ridden by Lester Piggott (aged seventeen), was late out of the stalls and, after passing the finishing post, slipped and threw his jockey. The horse was eventually caught a mile away by a stable lad.

Tulyar's seven victories were worth £75,173 10s. This was the most a single horse had ever earned in the history of British racing. It was also a record for the stock of his sire Tehran. Tulyar's trainer was Marsh, and Smirke was the jockey in six of the most valuable races.

The Grand National was held on 5 April. Although the BBC had broadcast the race for the previous twenty-five years, 1952 was to be rather different. Because of a copyright dispute, the lessees and managers of the Aintree Racecourse provided the commentary instead. This was transmitted by the BBC a few seconds after it was recorded. The commentators (four men and a woman) were not sufficiently experienced and made mistakes.

The 1952 Grand National winner was Teal, a horse that had once changed hands for £22 and had only had its first race in 1951. It was owned by Lane, trained by Crump and ridden by Thompson. It was in the first two from the start and won by five lengths; Legal Joy and Wot No Sun were second and third.

Ascot was held as usual although those taking part in the royal procession (17 June) were in half mourning. The royal party nevertheless attended every day all day, staying until after the last race. The Ascot Gold Cup was easily won by Aquino II. Owned by the Maharani of Baroda, the horse was trained by Armstrong at Newmarket and ridden by Gordon Richards. This was one of Richards' 231 winners in 1952, making him champion jockey for the twenty-fifth time.

THE OLYMPICS

It was an Olympic year with the VIth Winter Games taking place in Oslo (February) and the XVth Olympiad in Helsinki (July). Britain participated in both events. The most significant British performer at Oslo was the ice figure-skater Miss Jeanette Altwegg (aged twenty-two). She already held the British, World and European titles and now won the Olympic gold medal for women's ice skating with 161.760 points – the last time Britain had won this was in 1908. Following this latest success she announced her retirement from competitive skating and her intention to take up child welfare work.

Helsinki was to have hosted the Olympic Games in 1940 but the war intervened and instead the Finns were awarded the Games for 1952. Some sixty-nine nations (6,000 competitors) participated and as part of the preparations two villages were constructed – one for teams from behind the Iron Curtain, the other for teams from the rest of the world. There were eighteen events over sixteen days. At the end Sigfrid Edstrom (Sweden) retired as President of the International Olympic Committee and was replaced by Avery Brundage (USA).

Before leaving for Helsinki, the British and Commonwealth teams were received by the queen at a special tea-party at Buckingham Palace. The Duke of Edinburgh was in Helsinki for much of the games. The only British gold medal was gained on the very last day. It was won in the equestrian team event with Lieutenant-Colonel Harry Llewellyn on his horse Foxhunter (which he had ridden in the 1948 London Olympics), Stewart on Aherlow and White on Nizefella. There were also two silver medals (yachting; women's high jump) and eight bronze medals (3,000 metres; 100 metres; freestyle heavyweight wrestling; women's long jump; women's breast-stroke; cycling; hockey; women's relay). In the rowing events Britain reached five finals for the first time, but in every case the crews finished fourth.

Olympic horseman Harry Llewellyn, owner and rider of Foxhunter.

NINE

Transport, the Press, Science and National Service

FAREWELL TO THE LONDON TRAM

It was George Francis Train who introduced the tram to London in 1861. Originally horse-drawn, the system was electrified in the early twentieth century and supplemented by the trolleybus in the 1930s. It was also at that time (1933) that the London Passenger Transport Board ('London Transport') took over responsibility for the system from the London County Council (LCC). London Transport soon began to make preparations for phasing out the tram but although some services were ended, the Second World War and its aftermath gave trams an extended lease of life. So it was in July 1950 that London Transport published detailed plans for the withdrawal of the capital's remaining trams over the following two years and their replacement by buses.

The first of the (original) nine-stage 'Operation Tramaway', as it was known, began on 30 September 1950 when, among others, certain tram routes operating out of the depot at Wandsworth, south London, were withdrawn. As with the other early stages, some of the vehicles were allocated for use elsewhere on the network but most were to be broken up. Trams began to be scrapped on the following Monday, although a few were adapted for use on the site as a canteen and cloakroom. Soon afterwards another tram was acquired by Leeds Corporation and subsequently preserved at the Crich Tramway Museum.

The south London routes had survived twelve years longer than most of those operating in north London and so the sense of loss south of the river was greater. Loyalty to a service which had seen the people through the difficult days of the war generated much emotion and ceremony at each stage of the Tramaway programme. The tram/bus conversion in Croydon and Streatham (April 1951) typified this. London Transport used two 'doomed' trams, aware that many of their fittings and fixtures would disappear on the last day. The Croydon and Purley Chamber of Commerce hired both for a while to carry members of the Streatham Ratepayers Association. Money from the deliberately exorbitant fares (5s) went to charity.

LAST TRAM YEAR

At the beginning of 1952 there were fewer than 300 trams to serve eleven routes and these were further reduced in early January and April. The last tram went through the Kingsway Subway, Holborn, on Saturday 5 April. It was packed and those who travelled on it witnessed the ceremonial closing of the southern portal as the tram made its last run through the subway and back to Highgate. This ended Holloway's association with trams and the subway gates were opened a few hours later for them to serve in south London for a little longer. The subway was not considered suitable for use by buses and was closed for some years.

LAST TRAM WEEK

London Transport decided in 1952 to amalgamate the final two stages of withdrawal and announced that the last trams would run on the night of Saturday 5 July. Special commemorative tickets were

Lambeth's last tram, 5 April 1952. Mayor Elsie Boltz is seen in her fur coat saying goodbye to no. 33 (*Wandsworth Photographic*).

issued showing George Train's original vehicle alongside a modern tram. London Transport publicised the remaining six routes, pointing out that 'Never again will you be able to ride on a London tram.'

On the last morning 160 trams were available for the remaining six services which operated mostly in south-east London, from the Embankment to Eltham, Westminster to Woolwich, to Lewisham and Lee, through Peckham and across to Abbey Wood. All were crowded during that sunny day, with many groups again hiring a tram. Some dressed in Edwardian costume, while others placed pennies on the tracks for tram wheels to leave a lasting mark.

THE LAST TRAM

Officially the last tram was number 1951 working route 40. It was scheduled to leave Woolwich at 11.54pm, arriving back at New Cross depot at 12.30am on Sunday 6 July. It carried London Transport's Chairman, Lord Latham, and his deputy, a former tram driver who took the vehicle into the depot. Speeches were made, photographs taken and London's tram era was pronounced over. But the last tram working route 72 had left Woolwich later than the official last tram. Because it had been mobbed by excited crowds and took a longer route back, it arrived at New Cross *after* the closing ceremonies. To save embarrassment, it did not enter the depot but went straight to the scrapyard. So was this the end? Well, not quite. Abbey Wood depot was still operating and the last tram there did not arrive until about 3am. Now the era was truly over . . . at least for the rest of the twentieth century.

ANNUAL VETERAN CAR RUN

Another celebration of transport, the London–Brighton veteran car run, took place on a wet Sunday in early November. This was a long-standing event initially held to celebrate the end of the Red Flag Act, which had in theory required motorists to travel at no more than 4 mph and to be preceded by a man carrying a red flag to warn all in its path. There were 163 vehicles in the line-up in 1952, and only eleven of these failed to start. The vehicles left in order of age, with the oldest first. Some 143 reached Brighton by 4pm – the time the race was declared to have ended. The winner was a Lanchester built in 1902. Among the participants was Stirling Moss, who was a passenger in a 1903 Cadillac.

THE FIRST DAYS OF THE COMET

A 1903 Richard-Brasier setting off from Hyde Park. The rally from London to Brighton commemorates the first such run which took place in 1896.

Although the name Comet was first associated with aircraft in the early 1930s, as the de Havilland (DH 106) Comet, it only really became a name on everyone's lips in 1952. Prototypes of this design had been ordered in May 1946. While other companies were active in the same field, it was this design which won the race. The Comet flew for the first time in July 1949. Less than a year later Comet 1, flown by John ('Cat's Eyes') Cunningham, established a Cairo–London speed record of 5 hours 39 minutes, with an average speed of 386.46 mph.

It was the British Overseas Airways Corporation (BOAC) which did so much to ensure the success of the Comet. It had agreed to purchase eight Comets in 1946. This order was increased and the Corporation took delivery of nine Comet 1s. The Comet's progress was monitored by the Flight Development Unit under Captain Alderson. There were several problems to be solved as the plane was breaking new ground in terms of speed and altitude. For instance, the jet aircraft consumed fuel at a higher rate. This presented a potential danger should it need to stack (i.e. be held) at a low altitude while waiting to land. This in turn meant that new operating techniques needed to be mastered.

Commercial flights using the Comet 1 started at the beginning of May. In the preceding month journalists were taken in a Comet to Rome for lunch and back on the same day. The single journey of 900 miles by conventional aircraft normally took between four and a half and five hours, depending on the wind. But that April the Comet (aided by a following wind, it must be admitted) reached the Eternal City in less than two and a half hours.

On the evening of 2 May BOAC inaugurated the world's first regular jet airliner service. The destination was Johannesburg, and the journey of some 6,724 miles was accomplished with stops at Beirut and Khartoum. There was a change of crew at each stop. Flying time was calculated at 18 hours 40 minutes out, and 15 minutes longer for the return. This was 5 hours less than previous flights. In all it would take 23 hours 40 minutes including stops. The first flight arrived two minutes early!

Facilities were impressive and the service even more so. There was a 'passenger vestibule' where stewardesses welcomed arrivals with nightbags. There were cupboards for coats, hats and light bags. Also on board were what were described as washrooms, powder rooms and toilets. There was a drinking fountain and (just above it) a small library. Passengers had seats with finger-tip control which could be fixed into 'a variety of positions'. Some had seats facing inwards to tables. Hot and cold meals were served and much was made of the stillness and quietness of the flight.

On 23 May the Queen Mother and Princess Margaret had a 4-hour flight in a Comet. Their journey took them 1,850 miles over France, Switzerland and Italy, travelling at 500 mph. All nine of de Havilland's Comet 1s were delivered to BOAC in October and the services using them enjoyed an impressive 80 per cent occupancy. Tourist class travel across the Atlantic was introduced and again proved quite popular, especially because of the lower fares.

But the Comet was not to be the success so many hoped it would be. The first signs of this, albeit not comprehended, were in October when a Comet in Rome failed to take off, coming to a halt beyond the end of the runway. There were no casualties. Less than six months later (March 1953) a Comet at Karachi airport failed to take off and all eleven on

board were killed. On the very day of the
first anniversary, the pilot of a
Singapore–London flight taking off from
Calcutta lost control. Again all passengers
and crew were killed. Other accidents were
to follow soon afterwards. A later Court of
Inquiry found that metal fatigue in the skin
of the aircraft at the corner of the window
was the cause. It could not withstand the
pressure. The disasters of 1953/4 did
tremendous harm to the British aircraft

industry as a whole and in part paved the way for Boeing's success.

Also launched at this time was British European Airways' 'new
pressurised 245 mph Elizabethan' service which flew direct from
London to several European cities and offered complementary hot
meals. Promotional literature also reminded readers that 'money
spent on a BEA fare *stays inside Britain*' (advertisement's emphasis).

AIRPORTS FOR THE FUTURE

London Airport (Heathrow) served the capital well but was already
deemed insufficient for the growing number of passengers/flights.
Luton airport opened in September 1952, but the search had been on
before then for a second airport to handle London's European and
short-haul air traffic. In 1952 the Ministry of Civil Aviation
announced its decision. The choice was Gatwick, which at the time
was a privately owned airport established just before the Second
World War. Some 27 miles from London, it was on the well-served
London–Brighton line. The choice met with a mixed response, but
the need for it was generally agreed.

There was also widespread discussion of the potential for
helicopter services for short-haul and possibly continental European
traffic. It was seen as quite an exciting venture and many felt that
greater use of such vehicles would reduce the need for vast airport
complexes. Early in 1952 details were released for a proposed airport
for helicopters ('Helidrome') in the heart of London. The design had
been instigated by an MP and was the work of two London architects.
It was to occupy a site over the north end of the River Thames at
Charing Cross and extend into the Embankment Gardens.

AND FINALLY . . . HIT AND MISS ON THE NO. 78

Route 78, Shoreditch to Dulwich, London, crossed Tower Bridge.
Often this might mean waiting while the bascules were raised to

The famous incident. Here is a reconstruction showing the bus that jumped.

allow a ship to pass under the bridge. But on 30 December 1952 a double-decker bus 'jumped' a 3-foot gap when the northern bascule began to rise *before* the road traffic had cleared the bridge. Its driver, Albert Gunton, later explained that he had suddenly seen the road in front of him appear to be sinking. In reality, the bus was being lifted by one half of the bridge. The other half was stationary as the bus crashed on to it. Mr Gunton experienced a slight injury, as did eight of his passengers. He subsequently received a £10 reward for his calmness in response to such an experience.

THE PRESS

Although most of the British press was under the control of a few newspaper groups, there was still quite a wide choice. There were eleven national newspapers, including the *Daily Herald*, *Morning Advertiser* and *News Chronicle*, which have subsequently ceased to be published. There were about the same number of Sunday newspapers and titles, including *Empire News*, *Reynolds's News*, *Sunday Dispatch*, *Sunday Graphic* and *Sunday Pictorial*. Many smaller circulation newspapers (especially local) and some periodicals closed during the year. But many households took two daily national newspapers and sales had risen from 138 million copies a week in 1938 to 228 million by the end of 1952.

Supplies of newsprint improved from the spring and by late August freedom of consumption was restored although limits remained on the number of pages in any one issue. More space was, however, made available to advertisers, and full-page advertisements were printed for the first time since the 1930s. The *Manchester Guardian* printed news on its front page for the first time – in recognition of the fact that its new national status meant that the local nature of the advertisements previously featured there were no longer considered appropriate. Key figures in the industry included Brendan (Viscount) Bracken, chairman of the *Financial Times*, and J.B. Morton ('Beachcomber') of the *Daily Express*. Editors included Hugh Cudlipp (*Sunday Pictorial*) and John Gordon (in an advisory capacity at the *Sunday Express*). Malcolm Muggeridge succeeded Kenneth Bird ('Fougasse') at *Punch*.

COMICS

Comics had been a feature of popular British culture since the late nineteenth century with the emergence of the *Boy's Own Paper* (and *Girl's Own Paper* a little later). Others had appeared subsequently. But there was growing unease over a new type of comic which children were known to be reading avidly. These were from America. Such comics had become more widely known as a result of US servicemen reading and circulating them during the Second World War, and a British market for them had begun to develop. They might be imported or (to save foreign exchange) printed in Britain.

The concern in 1952 was over the comics' content – which differed considerably from what parents had known as children in the interwar period. American comics tended, it was argued, to focus on violence, sex and racial hatred. In Western ('cowboy') stories, the women were as vicious and as violent as the men while the portrayal of sex 'left little in picture or captions to children's imagination . . . normal decent relationships between men and women are ignored'. Such extremism was, it was said, similarly evident in the tales of horror, science fiction, crime and war which they also featured. Stories depicted science being used to revive a (decomposing) dead wife while a war serial showed an American soldier using wire to strangle a North Korean. There was discussion too over whether comic stories about crime actually encouraged it. In 1952 there were fourteen motions concerning comics at the National Union of Teachers' annual conference while the Women's Institutes and the Magistrates' Association voiced their concern over access to such comics and the latter launched an inquiry into them. The Co-operative Wholesale

Society stopped printing them. The campaign against these comics was in part led by the National Council for the Defence of Children under Dr Simon Yudkin and continued for the next few years. In due course it secured the Children and Young Persons (Harmful Publications) Act which sought to prevent the 'dissemination of certain pictorial publications' to such members of society.

British comics in contrast were deemed to be more acceptable, especially the creations of the Revd Marcus Morris. He was responsible for *Girl*, *Swift*, *Robin* and above all the *Eagle*, which sold around a million copies a week in 1952. Here were the thrilling adventures of Colonel Daniel MacGregor Dare and his companion Albert Digby with the spaceship *Ranger*. Arthur C. Clarke (the future author of *2001: A Space Odyssey*) was employed as a technical adviser. There was also PC 49, a popular community policeman, who was in effect the comic's equivalent to PC Dixon of Dock Green. Killed in *The Blue Lamp* (1950) PC Dixon would be resurrected in a successful BBC television series which took his name. The characters and stories were positively sold as wholesome. Indeed, an advertisement of the time highlighted its clergyman editor. The *Eagle* also featured tales of space exploration and articles on sport, science and nature: its underlying ethos was 'a Christian philosophy of honesty and unselfishness . . . cheap second-rate comic strips distort a boy's sense of values'. The *Eagle* aimed to see that 'the Devil does not have all the exciting comics', rejecting violence, cheap sensationalism and the worship of the superman. There was also an Eagle Club while *Lion* and *Tiger* (with 'Roy of the Rovers') successfully emulated the *Eagle* format.

SCIENCE AND DISCOVERIES:
FORTS, FAKES AND FAST ASLEEP

This was an important year for archaeology with major digs in progress all over the country. At Stanwick, Yorkshire, the doyen of British archaeologists Sir Mortimer Wheeler showed that the impressive earthworks of the Brigantine stronghold belonged to the period of the Roman invasion. Other investigations in the north were made by Professor and Mrs Piggott who explored hill-forts in southern Scotland and by Grahame Clark whose work centred on the east Yorkshire mesolithic site at Seamer. There was also important work going on at Lullingstone Roman villa, Kent. Further afield, Michael Ventris deciphered Linear B, one of the ancient languages of Crete, which was in the form of a dialect of early Greek. Linear A recorded the original language of the Minoans and had been used by them mainly for administrative purposes. One other discovery was an announcement in November by Kenneth Oakley that tests on the jawbone of the 'Piltdown Man' proved it was a fake. Evidently an ape's jawbone had been doctored with a chemical to make it look ancient.

In biology, Alan Turing suggested that interactions between the strengths of various chemicals, which he called morphogens, determined the biological make-up of a given species or an individual. Thus morphogens determined the stripes of a zebra or the spots of a leopard. It was in this year too that Rapid Eye Movement (REM) in normal sleep was identified, although its connection with vivid dreams was only realised later.

Piltdown Man, the famous hoax. This is a plaster cast reconstruction of the relics. The black areas indicate the relics, the grey areas are casts of the relics in reverse (to match up the two sides) and the white areas are the logical extensions of the relics.

KEEPING CALM, CHANGING SEX AND GOING NUCLEAR (ACCIDENT INCLUDED)

In medicine Robert Wallace Wilkins discovered the first tranquilliser, reserpine, which he used to treat high blood pressure. In addition, what is considered to be the world's first sex-change operation also took place. It was performed on George Jorgenson, who thereafter wished to be known as Christine.

The first breeder reactor, producing plutonium at the same time as producing uranium, was built by the US Atomic Energy Commission. What is generally seen as the first accident at a nuclear reactor occurred at Chalk River in Canada when an error caused the nuclear core to explode. A group led by the Hungarian-American physicist Edward Teller developed the first thermo-nuclear device, to be known as the H-bomb. The first such bomb, which works by nuclear fusion, was exploded at the Eniwetok Atoll in the South Pacific in November. Glenn Seabird discovered einsteinium, an artificial element with the atomic number 99, in the debris of the first thermo-nuclear explosion.

TRANSISTORS AND COMPUTER MALFUNCTION

The first commercial product using transistors instead of vacuum tubes was introduced in 1952. The product involved was a hearing aid. Sony began working on a pocket-sized transistor radio which it brought to market three years later. The American television network CBS used a computer to predict the results of the US presidential election. Its prediction – a landslide win for Eisenhower – was correct but it was not believed by its operators. Therefore it was quickly reprogrammed – and wrongly predicted a close result.

1952 NOBEL PRIZEWINNERS

The Nobel Foundation was set up under the terms of the will of Alfred Nobel (1833–96), a Swedish chemist and engineer. The first prizes were awarded in 1901 for chemistry, physics, medicine, literature and peace. The value of each prize in 1952 was about 171,000 Swedish kroner (£11,408). There were no women prizewinners for this year and only twelve had ever been awarded at the time.

The Nobel prize for chemistry was won by two Britons – A.J.P. Martin (of the Medical Research Council, London) and R.L.M. Synge (Rowett Research Institute, Bucksburn, Scotland) – for their discovery of partition chromatography, a method of chemical analysis. Synge had studied classics before going into science. Martin had also changed direction, from engineering to biochemistry. This was primarily because of the influence of J.B.S. Haldane. Martin and Synge had worked together at the University of Cambridge and at the Wool Industries Research Association's laboratories at Leeds.

The physics prize went to two Americans – Felix Bloch (Stanford University) and Edward Purcell (Harvard) – for their work in nuclear physics. That for medicine also went to an American – Professor Wakeman, who had discovered streptomycin. The literature prize went to François Mauriac, the French author and journalist whose output included poetry and such novels as *Thérèse Desqueyroux* and *La Pharisienne*. Nearly all Mauriac's best novels evoke his native area, the Landes, in particular its pine forests and vineyards.

The peace prize was a late award and went to Dr Albert Schweitzer. He accepted the prize but was too busy to receive it. He wrote to the committee accordingly, adding that the money would be used to establish a leper colony next to his hospital at Lambarene, a missionary station on the Ogowe river in the Gabon, which was then part of French Equatorial Africa. He had been associated with the area since 1913. Dr Schweitzer's letter was subsequently published and more money for the colony was raised as a result.

With the exception of the peace prize, the winners were announced in November and the following month met for a banquet hosted by the King and Queen of Sweden. There was a silent toast in memory of Alfred Nobel and then the prizewinners made short speeches. Dr Schweitzer attended in 1954 to deliver the traditional Nobel lecture of acceptance. There was a torchlight procession to mark his arrival and he was described as 'the greatest figure of our time'. In his lecture he noted that 'we are becoming inhuman in proportion as we become superhuman . . . live in peace with every man. These words are not only for individuals but also for nations.'

DEFENDING THE NATION

The first test of a British atomic bomb took place successfully on the Monte Bello Islands west of Australia on 3 October 1952 under the scientific direction of Dr W.G. Penney of the Ministry of Supply and with the involvement of the Australian government. It took place in HMS *Plym*, a frigate of 1,370 tons, and was designed to assess the effect of an atomic bomb exploding in a harbour. It was filmed from HMS *Campania*. The ship was totally destroyed and a tidal wave was caused.

Newsmen watching from a hilltop on the Australian coast, about 65 miles from the test area, saw a flash, ball of fire and billowing cloud, and experienced a sharp atmospheric shock-wave about four minutes after the flash. The noise resembled prolonged thunder. Dr Penney was knighted on 23 October – the same day that the RAF announced that Britain had begun to produce atomic bombs and the requisite aircraft to deliver them. All future bombers would carry atom bombs. There was already considerable interest in the use of nuclear energy for powering submarines and a homing torpedo was being developed that would follow and destroy its target no matter what evasive action it took.

Dr Albert Schweitzer, recipient of the Nobel Peace Prize in 1952.

ROB   *RIP 1952*

Rob, 'the paradog' was a black and white mongrel with a patch over one eye who had acted as a wartime parachute dog. He had served with the SAS and took part in landings in North Africa and Italy, including one drop behind enemy lines. He made over twenty parachute drops in various areas and seemed to enjoy jumping out of a plane. On landing he would remain still until his handler was able to remove his parachute. He received the Dickin Medal which was awarded by the People's Dispensary for Sick Animals (PDSA) and engraved with the words 'For Gallantry. We also Serve.' This has been called the animal kingdom's VC, only being awarded for exceptional bravery.

Members of the Gloucestershire Regiment arriving back from the Korean War aboard the troop ship *Empire Fowey*.

Conscription (known as National Service) was a feature of British life until 1963 – the first and only time (except for a few months before the outbreak of the Second World War) that such a scheme had operated in peacetime. Under the National Service Bill of March 1947, every male citizen aged between eighteen and twenty-six was liable for eighteen months' compulsory military service. Opposition was such, however, that the eventual Act reduced it to one year. But subsequent amendments, especially as a result of the outbreak of the Korean War, meant that National Service in 1952 was for two years, followed by three and a half years in the reserves.

Although National Service applied to every section of the community, there were exemptions, including blind people and clergymen. National Service could also be deferred by apprentices and those in higher education until they had completed their courses. But more significantly in terms of the numbers involved, those in certain jobs could defer their National Service indefinitely. Those affected were coalminers, oil shale underground workers, merchant sailors, seagoing fishermen and agricultural workers in essential food production. Graduate science teachers and police cadets could also defer and, like the others who did the same, found that in reality they had been exempted.

Conscientious objectors would appear before a local tribunal and would normally be excused military service on condition that they either undertook military service in a non-combatant unit (such as the Royal Army Medical Corps) or did community service instead. Once registered as a conscientious objector, the person concerned had to attend a military medical examination. Those who did not attend this would be arrested and imprisoned for six months. Conscientious objectors accounted for less than half of 1 per cent of conscripts in 1952 but often achieved considerable attention. One of

the most celebrated at this time was Michael Grieve, the son of the poet Hugh MacDiarmid. He objected to British policy in Kenya and argued that conscription was contrary to the Act of Union between England and Scotland which had been passed in 1707. But in June 1952, after a long legal battle, Glasgow Sheriff Court sent him to prison for six months. In Wales some men refused to complete their call-up papers in any language but Welsh.

A homosexual could state his sexual preferences at registration and seek exclusion from military service. It was a military offence for servicemen to be practising homosexuals. But medical and psychiatric opinion at this time viewed homosexuality as a perversion which National Service would cure. In reality long-standing homosexual relationships might be tolerated, especially in the Royal Navy, provided they were not prejudicial to service morale and discipline. But all too often homosexuals, particularly in the army, had to mask their orientation to avoid verbal or even physical abuse.

Four British soldiers kiss their fiancées goodbye as they leave to fight in Korea, December 1952.

On a lighter note, design and technology were about to make their impact on life in the Navy, Army, Air Force Institute – better known as the NAAFI. This was a club room with a bar and often a piano, and most offered hot meals, cigarettes, sweets and toilet requisites for sale. However, while the piano was a focal point, especially of an evening, it could easily be damaged by the beer glasses and cigarettes that were rested on it. The canteens began to take delivery of pianos built to overcome these problems. Cased in solid oak, the instrument was now to have a steeply pitched top with no place for beer glasses to stand, plastic keys which meant cigarette burns left only a small stain, wide pedals which made it difficult to overturn and a beer board, wider than the lid, to prevent liquor dripping in.

CIVIL DEFENCE AND THE RETURN OF DAD'S ARMY

Civil defence was an integral part of Britain's defence plans. There was the opportunity for part-time voluntary involvement (about five hours per month) in one of four organisations. These were the Special Constabulary, the Auxiliary Fire Service, the Civil Defence Corps and the National Hospital Service Reserve. Civil Defence instructors were trained at residential technical schools under the control of the Home Office. In December the Civil Defence Tactical School was opened by the Home Secretary, Sir David Maxwell Fyfe. It had been built in the grounds of the Civil Defence Staff College at Sunningdale to train officers who would be in control of operations at or near damaged areas. Among the features was a model of how Sheffield would look after the explosion of a large-scale atomic bomb. First aid instructors were mainly provided by the St John Ambulance Brigade, the British Red Cross and (in Scotland) the St Andrew's Ambulance Association.

The Home Guard was back, under legislation passed in 1951. It was open to all men aged between eighteen and sixty-five unless they were in the regular forces, certain reserves or the territorial army. Women were welcome to join as clerks or telephonists. Service in the Home Guard was for two years and could be extended one year at a time. It was voluntary and part time. There was no pay and little evidence of publicity or participation – recruiting posters were said to be collectors' items.

TEN

Outside the Norm: Women, Criminals and Immigrants

THE POSITION OF WOMEN: THE WORKPLACE

Despite contributing to the winning of two world wars, securing the vote in parliamentary elections and making some gains from legislation since 1918, women in Britain were still not equal citizens in 1952. This was evident in both political and economic terms and few advances were made during the course of the year. But there was little activity on the part of women to remedy this situation. Unlike the situation after the First World War, generally speaking women were able after the Second to hold on to paid employment if they wished, albeit government subsidies for day nurseries had been halved in 1945 and were withdrawn in 1946.

Women retained their economic significance because of the vital importance which the export drive assumed after 1945. They were required in particular to produce cotton, rayon and nylon for export. Furthermore, partly because National Service reduced the male workforce, they were also to be found in the transport, footwear and iron and steel sectors. Similarly the Women's Land Army had continued until 1950. Changes in technology and the beginnings of the consumer boom of the 1950s also created new job opportunities, particularly in light engineering. Above all the growth of the service economy both nationally and locally as a result of the welfare state and the expansion of retailing and financial institutions offered further opportunities for women to work, irrespective of age or marital status. In 1952 less than a third of women employed were under twenty-one while over a fifth of married women worked outside the home. Many of these did so part time because it suited them and their employer in a period of (in effect) full employment.

Even so, some jobs might still be closed to women. One woman who applied several times for work as a welder (a job she had done during the Second World War) used her initials and omitted her title on the application forms. She said that she would normally be

A Clydeside family enjoying their high tea, 1952.

interviewed but on each occasion, although told that she was the best qualified for the position, she was not taken on because she was unacceptable to the workplace as a woman. Other women might fail to advance as far as men because the higher posts in question 'naturally' were for men or advertised as such. Such discrimination was not outlawed until 1975.

The pattern which was emerging in 1952 nevertheless was for more and more women to work before and in the first years of marriage, breaking off only to bring up children until they reached school age. The reason for working might be economic need or to raise the family's standard of living in terms of owning (not renting) a home, a car or the latest kitchen appliances. During its first year of office the Conservative government reduced food subsidies, but reduced too income tax and the hire purchase restrictions on the purchase of vacuum cleaners, refrigerators and washing machines. The demands on some women – paid work, home and child care – were increasing, although the material rewards in particular were seen as worth it.

Studies in 1952, however, showed that many men did not pass on to their wives as large a proportion of their income as it was supposed they did. In particular the financial burden of having an extra child did not always fall on the family as a whole but on the mother and previous children. Furthermore, in a period of full employment and inflation, non-working wives often suffered a cut in real income as their housekeeping money was not increased (sufficiently). This might be partially offset by food subsidies, family allowances, school meals and the National Health Service (which at least was part financed by husbands heavily taxed on the drink and tobacco which they consumed). Finally a wife's expenditure on herself would normally come out of the housekeeping money or she would have to ask her husband for the amount required for (say) a new dress. Some women, especially if they had been financially well off before marriage, found this situation increasingly unacceptable and derived much satisfaction from regaining their economic independence.

WOMEN, MARRIAGE AND CHILDREN

Other women were content to enjoy what they saw as the joys of domesticity and child rearing which marriage frequently brought. That institution continued to gain in popularity but the postwar baby boom had already passed its peak by 1952. This was despite government encouragement for larger families (child allowance was only paid on the second and subsequent births) and the claim by the Archbishop of Canterbury to the Mothers' Union in 1952 that 'a family only truly begins with three children'.

The government's view (reflecting that of society generally) that most women would marry and have children was embodied in the National Insurance legislation. Married women did not need to pay such insurance (the 'stamp') as any entitlement to benefit would derive from their husbands' insurance record. There was only limited protest about this dependency status and no change of government policy. If married women did opt to pay National Insurance the rate of benefit was lower.

In the early 1950s a larger proportion of the population was married than in the past. The minimum age for marriage was sixteen in Britain. In Northern Ireland it had been fourteen for boys and twelve for girls until it was raised for both to sixteen in December 1951. Parental consent for marriage under twenty-one was required in England and Wales but not in Scotland. Sixteen-year-olds could marry there without such consent, and in 1952 those from outside Scotland who wished to marry without parental consent made the trip to Gretna Green accordingly. Public notice of marriages was required (hence 'calling the banns' in a church) unless a Special Licence was issued. A licence granted by the Archbishop of Canterbury cost £25. In 1952 men tended to marry at or before twenty-three, women at about twenty-one. Certainly almost half of all women aged between twenty and twenty-four were married.

CONTRACEPTION AND ABORTION

The Royal Commission on Population had recommended in 1949 that the National Health Service (NHS) should provide contraception information to married couples. But this did not happen until the 1960s, although by 1952 the Family Planning Association often held clinics on NHS premises. Both natural and artificial birth control were widely practised by this time though it was still formally discouraged by the Church of England (until 1958) and forbidden by the Catholic Church.

Eva PERON   RIP 1952

'Senorita Radio' was a stage, radio and film actress who was born in 1919 and met Juan Domingo Peron in December 1943 when he was in the Argentine Ministry of War. She married him in 1945 and was involved in his campaign to become president. In a country where women did not have the vote, no woman had done this before. Soon after he became president, she emerged as a powerful figure in shaping government policy. Her vast social aid fund, her championship of Los Descamisados ('the shirtless ones') and her demand for women to have the right to vote won her much support, along with much middle- and upper-class hostility. In 1951 she withdrew her candidature for the vice-presidency because of opposition from the army. Her failing health was temporarily reprieved with an operation in November 1951. She made her last public appearance at the inauguration of her husband's second presidential term, dying soon afterwards at the age of thirty-three.

A chemist's shop in the 1950s. The cigarette machine outside was a normal part of street furniture at the time, as was the milk machine on the left.

The church's stance may have had little practical effect but it did mean that many people felt guilty or at least uneasy about practising birth control. Traditionally the man was seen as being responsible for preventing unwanted pregnancies and the latex condom, which was a principal form of male contraception, had first been produced in England in the interwar period. But many men were against using them and there remained something furtive about securing supplies even by those who were willing to do so. Pharmacies, especially national chains, might refuse to stock them. Many purchasers looked to the barber to make the first move, to pose the vague question 'Something for the weekend, Sir?' or else muttered the request along with other items in the hope that no one else would notice. But developments in 1952 were in due course to change this with the first manufacture of a contraceptive tablet of phosphorated hesperidin.

Induced abortion had been illegal since 1861 unless the life of the mother was in danger. Private nursing homes might offer safe abortions but these were too costly for most of those who needed their services. Back-street abortionists or self-administered (but often unreliable or dangerous) remedies were the usual way out for the unmarried or married woman carrying an unwanted child.

DIVORCE

The divorce rate had increased significantly after the war. In 1938 under 7,000 divorces had been granted in Britain; there were over 60,000 in 1947. As a result the government set up the Denning Committee on Procedure in Matrimonial Cases which recommended in 1948 that divorce be made easier to overcome the administrative backlog. It also urged support for marriage through such organisations as the Marriage Guidance Council, founded in 1938. The Catholic Church, which did not allow divorce, opened marriage counselling centres in Birmingham, Bristol and Liverpool during the course of the year.

Generally speaking, divorce was only granted after a minimum of three years' marriage. Grounds for divorce were adultery by the respondent since marriage or at least three years' desertion by the respondent immediately before the petition. Cruelty, insanity (under certain conditions) and the commission by the husband of certain criminal sexual offences might also lead to the granting of a divorce. Legal aid for divorce first became available in 1950. In 1952 some 36,000 divorces were made absolute. Most of these were on the grounds of adultery or desertion but over 14 per cent were because of cruelty. Over three-quarters of those who divorced remarried. They rarely enjoyed the blessing of the church, however, as it was contrary to Catholic teaching and second marriages were seen as adulterous by the then Archbishop of Canterbury.

HOMOSEXUALITY

Homosexuality, even in private between consenting adults, was illegal and an active (or even suspected) homosexual frequently faced violence or blackmail and loss of employment. But the number of people actually brought to court varied considerably. In 1938 the number of men prosecuted for homosexual offences was under 1,000; in 1952 it was almost 4,000. This was primarily because of the increased determination to bring such men to trial. In October 1952 the Home Secretary told the House of Commons that homosexuals were exhibitionists, proselytisers and a danger to others. Such comments resulted in increased police action against homosexuals, especially if they were in the public eye. Among those to suffer in this way in the near future were a Labour MP and the actor John Gielgud.

John Gielgud (and Marlon Brando) in the film of *Julius Caesar*, made in 1952 (*MGM: courtesy Kobal*).

The view that homosexuality was a disease led to the imposition of 'cures' on those who were convicted. They were often required to undergo chemical or hormonal treatment and/or aversion therapy. However, some experts who saw homosexuality as a disease did begin to question whether that necessarily made it a crime. But it was only in the mid-1950s that the Wolfenden Committee was appointed, which was later to recommend that some homosexual activity be allowed. Lesbianism was not illegal and rarely entered public discussion.

CRIME, LAW AND ORDER

There were 159 separate police forces in Britain and they were classified as County Forces, Borough Forces, Combined Forces (whose areas of responsibility extended to neighbouring counties or boroughs), the Metropolitan Police Force and the City of London force. The largest was the Metropolitan, with nearly 20,000 police for a population of almost eight million; the smallest was a county in Scotland with fifteen officers. Generally speaking, the age of recruitment for those in England and Wales was between 19 and 30 for men and 20 to 35 for women; it was 20 to 30 for men in Scotland. The aftermath of the war was evident, however, in that ex-regulars over thirty from the armed services were eligible to join the force.

PRISONS

There were fewer than four thousand prison staff (all grades) and only 8 per cent were women. The inmates were separated by gender, as well as young persons from adults, the untried from the convicted and the civil from the criminal. Those sentenced to hang were also treated separately. Prisoners were likely to be given some remission, usually serving two-thirds of their sentence. Normally prisoners worked twenty-five hours per week. This time, which was paid, was spent according to what the prison could offer. There were prison workshops, farm work, domestic work and gardening. Education and culture featured in prison life. Evening classes, often with the participation of local education authorities, were held. There might also be lectures, films, concerts and drama.

Following the Criminal Justice Act (1948), those under twenty-one would only be sent to prison if there were no appropriate alternative. There were many such alternatives in 1952; for example, the remand home, which offered safe custody for boys and girls before or during appearance at court. It was in effect a short punitive detention centre. There were also Borstals and Approved Schools. The former took its name from a place in Kent where the first such institution was set up at the beginning of the century; by 1952 there were seventeen for boys and three for girls. The sentence could be anything between nine months and three years, but up to one year might be spent outside the institution under supervision. There were 130 Approved Schools in England and Wales. They provided education and training for young offenders and children.

Finally there were Detention and (new) Attendance Centres. Those aged between fourteen and twenty-one could be sentenced to the former, usually for three months. The aim, in the language of the time, was to give them a 'short, sharp shock' to make it clear that the law could not be defied with impunity. There were few Attendance Centres in 1952. Postwar priority in building to maintain law and order had been directed towards housing for police rather than offenders. The aim of the centres was that certain offenders should attend them in their spare time, where they would be provided with a suitable occupation and taught how to make proper use of their leisure.

Whipping offenders had been abolished four years before under the same criminal justice act. But there was still widespread support for this form of punishment. In November 1952 the magistrates in Manchester submitted a request to the Home Secretary that it be restored in view of the violence committed against old people, women and children, particularly in their own homes. No action resulted, and probation was often preferred. Both this and the general notion of after-care service can be said to date from the late nineteenth century. Probation had been heavily used in the interwar period and following an improvement in the recruitment of probation officers still played a major part in 1952. By then there were some 1,100 probation officers, most of whom were employed full time.

Interest in restoring whipping was indicative of the growing anxiety at this time over juvenile crime. Various explanations were offered – the effects of the Second World War on the breakdown of home and family life, the growing disrespect for law because of the black market and its contentious hero the spiv. A debate in the House of Lords in November 1948 on 'The increase in crime' had led to cooperation between the Home Office and the Ministry of Education in a programme which was still continuing in 1952 and which focused on prevention rather than detention through improved provision of local amenities and education in citizenship. But the popular view remained that the courts were letting too many miscreants off. But there were too often insufficient institutions, and some of the fines dated from 1879! One response was the 'fit person order' which for a while shifted responsibility for children to local authority homes. But they in turn, because of pressure on their resources, increasingly licensed such children back to their parents.

CRIMES CÉLÈBRES

Crimes which aroused considerable public interest in 1952 included the murder of a five-year-girl by John Straffen, who had escaped from Broadmoor (where he had been detained since the previous year for the murder of two other children), and the murder in August of Sir John and Lady Drummond and their young daughter while on holiday in the French Alps. In October there was a shooting incident at Knowsley Hall in Lancashire, the home of the Earl of Derby. Harold Winstanley, a young footman, shot dead two butlers and slightly wounded the Countess of Derby. The crimes which probably captured most attention, however, were the £200,000 post office mail van robbery off Oxford Street, London, in May and the murder of a Croydon policeman in November.

'LET HIM HAVE IT, CHRIS'

It was soon after 9pm on 2 November that PC Sidney Miles and Detective Officer John Fairfax along with other police officers responded to a 999 call. Two people had been seen at a warehouse belonging to Barlow & Parker in Tamworth Road, West Croydon, Surrey. The building was surrounded and the two individuals, later to be identified as Chris Craig (aged sixteen) and Derek Bentley (nineteen), in an effort to evade the police, headed on to the roof. But they were pursued and Miles and Fairfax led the chase. During the pursuit, Bentley was temporarily captured while Craig, still free, taunted them: 'Come on coppers. I'm only sixteen.' He added that his brother had recently been sent to prison for twelve years. Then shots were fired by Craig. According to police evidence given during the trial, Bentley was heard to say 'Let him have it, Chris.' As a result of this, though Bentley had already been captured, Fairfax was shot and wounded in the shoulder but PC Miles was killed instantly. Aged forty-two and the father of two children, PC Miles had been in the police service for twenty-two years. Craig and Bentley were eventually taken into custody.

Derek Bentley was an electrician from Norbury, Surrey. He was charged with being concerned with Christopher Craig in the murder of PC Sidney Miles. Bentley's response was: 'Craig shot him. I have not got a gun. He was with me on the roof and shot him then between the eyes.' Bentley subsequently appeared before Croydon magistrates but made no reply when formally charged; Craig was in Croydon General Hospital because of injuries received in a fall but he was also to face the same charge.

The trial took place on 9–11 December before Lord Chief Justice Goddard. Both defendants pleaded not guilty to the charges. Christmas Humphries led the prosecution case, arguing that Bentley had incited Craig to begin the shooting. Even though the former was technically under arrest at the time Miles was killed, he was party to the murder and equally responsible in law.

During the course of the trial Craig's father, a bank official, explained that his son could neither read nor write. He was a gentle individual who had attended Bible class until two years before and had only withdrawn for fear of being asked to read. Since then he had become fond of reading comics and seeing films. Both Craig and Bentley denied that the words 'Let him have it, Chris' had ever been uttered.

With the trial over, the jury retired for just over an hour. They returned a verdict of guilty but with a recommendation of mercy in the case of Bentley. Lord Goddard agreed when submitting details to the Home Secretary but added that he thought Craig was one of the most dangerous young criminals ever to appear in the dock. He had in mind the boy's taunts that he was only sixteen and knew that whatever happened he would escape the death penalty because of his youth. His brother's recent sentence meant that he hated the police.

Despite the plea for mercy Bentley was condemned to death. There was widespread unease, indeed hostility, over whether he should hang. A campaign for a reprieve was launched but lost. On the night before the execution the Speaker refused to allow the matter to be debated. A small, all-party group of MPs sought out Sir David Maxwell Fyfe, the Home Secretary, for one last plea. Finally a group of demonstrators marched on his chambers in the Temple. Nevertheless Bentley was hanged on 28 January 1953. Earlier that month Detective Sergeant Fairfax had been awarded the George Cross for the bravery shown in the arrest of the two teenagers. Despite subsequent campaigning by his family, Derek Bentley was not to receive a pardon until almost the end of the century.

Lord Justice Goddard.

IMMIGRANTS

The Labour government's Economic Survey for 1947 concluded that 'foreign labour can make a useful contribution to our needs. . . . This need to increase the working population . . . is a permanent feature of our national life.' The largest postwar group of immigrants to Britain were the Irish. They came because of the relative economic and social stagnation of their own country in the aftermath of the war years, although the future Irish republic had remained neutral. Britain was again a land of opportunity, particularly because of the rebuilding which was now about to begin. But they often faced discrimination – the notice proclaiming 'Rooms to let' was often (and legally) supplemented by the message 'No Irish'.

There were also the European Volunteer Workers and the Polish Resettlement Corps. Between 1945 and 1950 some 100,000 Polish refugees and 85,000 Italians and eastern Europeans were recruited for British industry. As 'aliens' they could be directed to priority areas. If they left a job without permission they could be deported to a camp for displaced persons on the continent. Certainly many had left by the early 1950s to seek opportunities elsewhere, notably the USA, because of various difficulties which they had encountered in Britain.

By 1951 the British and continental economies were relatively buoyant again and there were few new European workers coming to the UK. But the labour shortage remained, as the king's speech in October that year had made plain. By now the Nationality Act of 1948 had given all British subjects of the Commonwealth and Empire the free and unrestricted right to live and work in Britain. It cost the West Indians about £100 each for the journey to Britain. Yet the 1951 census shows that only about 15,000 people born in the West Indies were resident in Britain, 4,000 of them in London.

Generally speaking, the national press paid little attention to this small community and neither industry nor government was enthusiastic about encouraging their presence. In June 1948 the troopship *Empire Windrush* had arrived at Tilbury with 492 Jamaicans aboard. It was well received. The London *Evening Standard* spoke of those passengers who had served in the British forces during the Second World War as returning to 'the Motherland'. Jobs were found for the 202 skilled men immediately and others were also to find employment soon. But although a couple of hundred more arrived during the course of each of the next few years there was little desire to encourage widespread movement within the Empire. The Board of Trade (which governed the textile industry) opposed the recruitment of Jamaican women, despite a shortage of 43,000 workers in the industry. They argued that such women would be illiterate and unable to withstand the Lancashire climate. The London County Council refused to employ Bermudan women in its hospitals. But gradually more came: 1,000 in 1951 and 2,000 in 1952. The latter increase was in part a response to the McCarren-Walter Act of that year which restricted West Indian immigration to the USA.

The welcome was less warm in 1952. The 'Mother Country' was less accommodating to West Indians, Indians and Pakistanis than their English-centred education and the ideals of late Empire had led them to believe. Already the newcomers were, like the Irish and others before them, facing covert (if not overt) discrimination. 'No

These Jamaicans have just reached the 'land of hope' aboard the *Empire Windrush*.

coloureds' was added to 'No Irish'. Such attitudes extended to accommodation, employment, even church membership. While the British Christian Church did not support racial discrimination, parishioners often showed their unease over the presence of the new arrivals who obligingly did not return. These immigrants began to be viewed as presenting something of a (unspecified) 'problem'. The problem of discrimination on the part of the host community was recognised by government but only informal voluntary measures were proposed to overcome it.

Chaim WEIZMANN   *RIP 1952*

Weizmann was a distinguished chemist and champion of the Zionist cause. He played an important part in securing the Balfour Declaration (1917) which argued for a 'National Home for Jews'. When the independent state of Israel was founded in 1948 he was elected its first president, a post he held until his death.

A World Away

THE ISLE OF MAN AND THE CHANNEL ISLANDS

The Isle of Man had a population of 55,000 at this time, over a third of whom lived in the capital, Douglas. The Lieutenant Governor at the beginning of the year was Air Vice-Marshal Sir Geoffrey Bromet. In September he was succeeded by Sir Ambrose Dundas. There had been a general election the previous year which had returned eighteen Independents for the 24-member House of Keys. Agriculture remained the predominant activity and there was a major programme under way to free the island's herds of bovine tuberculosis.

There was growing interest and awareness of the island's heritage. In 1952 the National Trust of England and Wales handed over the Calf of Man on a long lease to the Manx National Trust and three medieval buildings – the thirteenth-century chapel of St Mary in Castletown, the fourteenth-century Friary Chapel of Bemaken, Kirk Arbory, and the three-arched pack-horse bridge at Kirk Malew – were restored. Looking to the future, however, work was almost complete for the new airport.

The Channel Islands form Britain's only remaining part of the Duchy of Normandy. They comprise Jersey, Guernsey, Alderney, Sark and Herm. They make up an area of 75 square miles and in 1952 had a total population of under 100,000. Their potato and tomato crops were high this year but, as with mainland Britain, there was an outbreak of foot and mouth disease. Among the highlights of 1952 was the proclamation of the queen's accession and a visit by the Duke and Duchess of Gloucester. Some 4,000 heard the proclamation in the Royal Square in St Helier and there was a special sitting of the States of Jersey. Members paid tribute to King George VI and referred (rightly) to the new monarch as the Duchess of Normandy. There was a visit by the Duke and Duchess of Gloucester to mark the centenary of Victoria College and the sale by Britain of 1,000 acres of Alderney which it had used for military purposes since the mid-nineteenth century.

NORTHERN IRELAND

Northern Ireland, with a population of almost 1.4 million, had its own parliament and Executive, together with twelve MPs at Westminster.

The Governors of the Province in 1952 were Earl Granville, who had held the post since September 1945, and Lord Wakehurst, who succeeded him in December. The prime minister was Viscount Brookeborough of Colebrooke (formerly Sir Basil Brooke), who held the post from 1943 to 1963.

The province's budget for this year provided for an increased contribution to the British exchequer and legislation was also passed for the same new allowances, benefits and charges in health and social services to operate as prevailed on the mainland. But controversy remained over the discriminatory treatment of Catholics in housing, education and employment. The convention at this time was that such matters should not be raised in the British House of Commons. There was no Secretary of State for Northern Ireland until 1972.

Economically speaking it was a mixed year, with recession in the textile industry only partly offset by the Ministry of Supply placing shirt orders worth £1.2 million with twenty-three Northern Ireland firms. The Belfast shipping industry was in a reasonable state having in 1951 taken second place in the world for tonnage output from a single shipbuilding yard.

Ulster Premier Viscount Brookeborough takes his seat in the Lords, 12 November 1952.

THE REPUBLIC OF IRELAND

The Republic of Ireland had only adopted that name at Easter 1949, having been known as the Irish Free State since its formation in 1922. The change followed legislation a few months earlier at about the same time that it withdrew from the British Commonwealth of Nations. These moves ended the country's last formal links with the UK, although it continued to remain in the Sterling Area. The

British government's reaction, as embodied by the Ireland Act (1949), was to declare 'that in no event will Northern Ireland or any part thereof cease to be part . . . of the United Kingdom without the consent of the Parliament of Northern Ireland'. Dublin did not welcome this guarantee by the Attlee government and that led to the Republic's sudden decision, without consultation, to leave the Commonwealth.

In 1952 the president of the Irish Republic was Sean T. O'Kelly. Known affectionately as 'Sean T', he was re-elected unopposed for a second seven-year term. The Taioseach (prime minister) was Eamon de Valera. The Republic, which was neutral throughout the Second World War, also chose to remain outside the North Atlantic Treaty Organisation (NATO; founded 1949) and said that this would be its policy while the partition of the island lasted.

The country faced some economic trouble over budget deficits and the cost of living rose by 18 per cent during the period February 1951–July 1952. Nevertheless, the government decided to end all food rationing in the Republic. Bread, butter, flour, sugar and tea were now freely available for unlimited purchase. At the same time, subsidies on flour and bread were reduced while those on butter, sugar and tea were ended. Agriculture, the country's main employer, had a prosperous year. Furthermore, while there was an overall trade deficit, exports to Northern Ireland and Britain exceeded imports for the first time.

In cultural terms, events of the year included a production of *Hamlet* which was performed by the Dublin Gate Theatre Company at the scene of the play's action, the Castle of Elsinore in Denmark. Plans were made for a new Abbey Theatre in Dublin following the destruction by fire of the previous one in 1951. Plans too were made for An Tostal – Ireland's national festival which aimed to rival that at Edinburgh.

BRITISH EMPIRE AND COMMONWEALTH

The term British Empire was still in regular use although the term (British) Commonwealth of Nations was gaining increasing currency at this time. Its members were to be found throughout the five continents. India was the only republic in the Commonwealth, with a mix of titles for all the other territories. The Dominions, each with its own Governor-General appointed by the monarch, in 1952 comprised Ceylon, Pakistan, the Union of South Africa, Canada, the Commonwealth of Australia and New Zealand. Within the Empire itself there were colonies, some of which were self-governing, protectorates, mandates and a condominium.

Vincent Massey, the first Canadian-born Governor-General of Canada, 29 January 1952.

Indian Prime Minister
Jawaharlal Nehru.

INDIA AND THE DOMINIONS

India, even then noted as the world's largest democracy, completed the first elections to the lower house, which had begun a few months before, in early 1952. The prime minister was Nehru. The death of independent Ceylon's first prime minister in a horse-riding accident was a great shock. He was succeeded by his son. Canada secured the first appointment of its own national Vincent Massey as Governor-General in succession to Viscount (later Earl) Alexander of Tunis. This was a new development in Dominion government, but was not emulated by New Zealand or Australia, which, in selecting Sir Willoughby Norrie and Field Marshal Sir William Slim respectively as the queen's representatives, maintained the older tradition of the appointment being made and decided by what many in those lands still considered to be the 'Mother Country'.

SOUTH AFRICA

This was a particularly significant year for South Africa. In the general election of May 1948 the Afrikaner National Party had championed the policy of apartheid, of separation between whites and non-whites. The victory of the National Party under Dr Malan led to its introduction. Racial segregation, practised in South Africa since the start of colonisation, was intensified and the apparatus to guarantee white Afrikaner supremacy in the Transvaal was extended to other areas of the Union.

> ## 2nd Marquess of LINLITHGOW   RIP 1952
>
> Born in 1887 and educated at Eton, he was the son of the first Governor General of Australia. Active in Conservative Party politics following service in the First World War, he became involved in Indian affairs. In April 1936 he was appointed Viceroy of India, a position he held until early 1943. He secured India's participation in the Second World War and the provision of a volunteer army of two million. But because of the Muslim League's insistence upon partition, he was unable to maintain the country's unity. Its division became increasingly inevitable in the last years before independence.

World hostility to the policy began to be voiced in 1952, notably by the United Nations General Assembly, and its development dominated both the South African parliament and courts which saw a prolonged constitutional crisis for most of that year (and beyond). On 20 March, in the case of Harris v. Minister of the Interior, five judges of the appellate division of the South African Supreme Court unanimously held invalid the act passed by the South African parliament altering the franchise of those who were then termed Cape Coloured voters. The judgment was based on the fact that the legislation did not have the required two-thirds majority. The government rejected its legal implications and the parliament passed a new act designed to avoid the legal consequences of the court's ruling. A High Court of Parliament was established under an act of that name. Boycotted by opposition parties, this met and set aside the appeal court's decision.

The same litigant, the Coloured voter G. Harris, had, however, contested the High Court of Parliament Act itself. Three judges of the Cape provincial division of the Supreme Court held that this act too was invalid. The government appealed against the decision to the appellate division of the Supreme Court and lost. The government argued that parliament must be supreme while the opposition maintained that the rule of law, as interpreted by the ordinary courts, must be upheld. The issue was to feature prominently in the country's general election held in 1953, and the victory of the National Party saw further measures introduced.

The African National Congress, under James Moroka, and the South African Indian Congress, under Y.M. Dadoo, had decided in December 1951 to campaign jointly against racial discrimination. Dr Malan warned the Congress that disturbances would be 'dealt with'. On 6 April demonstrations were held coinciding with the van Riebeeck celebrations marking the tercentenary of white settlement in the Cape. The second phase began on 26 June with the breaking of various apartheid and pass laws. During the first three months of

Sympathisers shake hands with Nelson Mandela on the occasion of his arrest, with others, for defiance of the apartheid laws, 26 June 1952.

the campaign some 4,000 non-Europeans were arrested, and most were imprisoned. Opposition to the imposition of apartheid was often punished under anti-Communist legislation. A weekly newspaper, the *Guardian*, was declared to be Communist and was banned. Trade unions were under threat too, with the Industrial Legislation Commission recommending the strict separation of white and non-white workmen into different representative bodies.

South Africa's policy of apartheid had an impact on British policy in the area too. Generally speaking, the Labour Party had opposed racial discrimination. But in 1948, while in government, it placed expediency before principle. Seretse Khama, heir to the Bangwato chieftaincy in Bechuanaland (subsequently renamed Botswana; but then part of British South Africa Territories), chose to marry a white woman, Ruth Williams. Bowing to pressure from South Africa and fearing (it was said) hostility from the Bangwato tribe itself, Seretse was subsequently told that his headship would not be recognised. Furthermore, in 1950 he was exiled from the tribal reserve for five years. Patrick Gordon Walker, the Labour Secretary of State for Commonwealth Relations, wanted to ban all such mixed marriages.

In March 1952 it was announced in both Houses of the British parliament that the refusal to recognise Seretse as chief was permanent and that he could not return from exile until a successor had been appointed. On learning of this, Mr Anthony Wedgwood Benn MP proposed a debate on the issue as a matter of urgency. This was refused. The Bangwato sent a delegation to London but the decision was not rescinded. There were disturbances in the territory for most of the remainder of the year.

THE COLONIES

Churchill, while an enthusiast for empire, recognised on returning to office that the clock could not be turned back. Nevertheless, although India, 'the jewel in the crown', was independent, the government chose to represent the continuing transformation of Empire into Commonwealth as a success. It was argued that the process was a triumph of British statesmanship and that there was a long-established programme of preparing dependent states for self-government. Even so, the prevailing bipartisan sentiment in 1952 was that Britain's African Empire would continue for another few generations. Economic development and constitutional changes were deemed necessary before control could be ceded over these territories. During 1952 there were debates in the British House of Commons on closer association in Central Africa, on Kenyan land use and on general colonial affairs. Education was seen as essential to implement the move towards independence, and a conference was held in September at Cambridge under the chairmanship of Sir Philip Morris, vice-chancellor of Bristol University, to discuss this. Furthermore, while local educational facilities were increasing (colonial universities and university colleges had almost 3,500 students), those studying in the UK had increased from 300 in 1939 to over 5,000 at the beginning of 1952.

But if gradualism was believed to be the key for the future of the African colonies in London, there were those in the territories themselves who sought to be rid of white settlers and white control as soon as possible, and vigorously pursued policies to achieve this. The most substantial challenges in 1952 were in Kenya and Malaya.

KENYA

Kenya had been formed out of the East African Protectorate in 1920. The Kikuyu, the most powerful group of people in the vicinity of the capital, Nairobi, formed a political organisation known as the Kikuyu Central Association. This campaigned, among other things, for the restoration of land which they claimed had been unfairly taken from them by the Europeans. In 1929 a young representative of the association, Jomo Kenyatta, was sent to London to pursue the case and make contact with sympathetic Labour MPs. He was away from Kenya for most of the next seventeen years, making a living as a journalist, farmer – and as an extra in *Sanders of the River*.

By 1940 the Kikuyu people had emerged as the leaders of African resistance to white settler supremacy and, in effect, to British rule. The association was banned and its leaders in Kenya imprisoned. Kenyatta remained free, returning to Kenya in 1946 as something of a national hero. He was made head of the college at Githunguri, and this became an important base and inspiration for the future; he soon became a leader in the Kenyan African Union, which campaigned for greater political participation in the colony. Also in 1946 a secret Kikuyu society known as the Mau Mau began to operate. It was anti-European, anti-government and anti-Christian, and sought, by restoring ancient customs of oath-taking and murder, to drive white farmers and their labourers out of the traditional Kikuyu lands.

In April 1952, following a crime-wave attributed to the Kikuyu in Nairobi and other towns, five Kikuyu villages were collectively fined £2,500 for suppressing evidence in cases of hut-burning instigated by this society. In August the Nyeri and Nanyuki districts were placed under curfew. At the same time Kenyatta, alarmed at the rapid growth of the Mau Mau and hoping to achieve reform through

Jomo Kenyatta, leader of the Kenyan African Union, leaving court in handcuffs during his trial, 5 December 1952.

democratic means, addressed a crowd of around 30,000 at Kiambu. Here he cursed the Mau Mau with a powerful Kikuyu oath. The leaders of the Mau Mau summoned Kenyatta to remonstrate with him over this action: he did not denounce them again.

During September murders of anti-Mau Mau Africans and attacks on property increased. A state of emergency was declared soon after the arrival of the new governor, Sir Evelyn Baring, at the end of that month. The Kenya regiment and police reserves were mobilised and Home Guards formed. The Kenyan African Union was believed to be behind the Mau Mau and Kenyatta, along with other leaders, was arrested. The organisation was banned, more radical leaders took over and terrorism became more widespread. Europeans were attacked and killed for the first time.

Some 3,500 Kikuyu squatters were moved off European farms into the reserves and by the end of November 13,000 Kikuyu had been detained, of whom 2,000 were later released and 5,000 charged. Jomo Kenyatta was put on trial before the end of the year. The main accusations were that he had administered the Mau Mau oath, was insincere in denouncing the society and had allowed his name to replace that of Jesus Christ in hymns sung by the organisation. In an unfair trial – the presiding judge was bribed and the chief prosecution witness perjured himself – Kenyatta was found guilty and imprisoned until April 1959. He became prime minister of self-governing Kenya in 1963 and its president the following year.

MALAYA

In Malaya 1952 marked the fifth year of the Communist insurrection. This had begun in June 1948 when several thousand Communists, most of whom were Chinese, led by former members of the Malayan People's Anti-Japanese Army, took up arms against estate owners and rubber planters in an attempt to establish what they termed 'liberated areas'. The British responded by proclaiming a state of emergency and so began the 'jungle war' against the Malayan Races Liberation Army of Chen Ping, Secretary General of the Malay Communist Party. It lasted until 1960 but was particularly ferocious in the early 1950s.

The British resistance to the unrest in 1952 was led by the High Commissioner General Sir Gerald Templer. Following the killing of his predecessor in October 1951 and the retirement of Lieutenant Colonel Briggs in that December, Sir Gerald had overall control of both the civil administration and the military forces. He said in February that 'I would win this war in three months if I could get two-thirds of the people on my side'. In March, 128 terrorists were

General Sir Gerald Templer,
High Commissioner of Malaya,
on a tour of a new village,
26 August 1952.

killed, wounded or captured. This was the lowest total since January 1951. Casualties to the security forces were far higher. Life on British-owned rubber plantations and tin mines now resembled siege conditions – 6-foot high barbed-wire fences, Bren guns, dug-outs and guard posts were all common.

Among the victims of the terrorism was Michael Codner, Assistant District Officer at Tanjony Malim. During the Second World War he had been a prisoner in Germany. He escaped over a vaulting horse with his companion Eric Williams, who recorded their experience in *The Wooden Horse*. In August Sir Gerald ordered that the village of Permatung Tinggi be destroyed and some seventy of its inhabitants were detained for failing to give information after a Chinese official had been murdered by terrorists. He also established the Malayan Federation Regiment which was open to all racial communities. Conscription and national service in the police/civil defence organisations were now introduced. During the course of the year 1,135 terrorists were killed and over 300 taken in custody.

EGYPT

The British military presence in Egypt had begun in 1882. Although Britain had recognised Egypt's sovereign independence in 1922 the troops remained. In 1936 an Anglo-Egyptian treaty provided for the gradual withdrawal of the troops except from the Canal Zone, which was to remain under British protection because of financial interests and its importance as a waterway. The British departure was postponed by the Italian invasion of Egypt in 1940 and the troops were to remain continuously on Egyptian soil until 1956. Resentment against the British presence resurfaced after the end of the war and increased following hostility to the lifestyle of King Farouk. Military disillusion with the king followed the nation's failure in the war against Israel in 1948. To counter this the king appointed anti-British governments and in October 1951 the Egyptians unilaterally denounced the 1936 agreement.

These policy changes encouraged violence in the Canal Zone and in January a Cairo newspaper printed the offer of a £E1,000 reward for the assassination of Lieutenant-General Sir George Erskine, the British officer commanding the area. At the same time 'liberation units' entered the area and were active around Suez and on the road from Ismailia to Zagazig. On 12 January there was a serious engagement at Tel el-Kebir. The British response, including the occupation of villages used as operational bases by the guerrillas, led many of the liberation units to withdraw to Ismailia where there was a further attack on the British. On 25 January the British attacked a public building which they believed to have been the centre of terrorist activities in Ismailia. Nearly 800 Egyptians,

Ex-King Farouk and ex-Queen Narriman in exile on Capri, August 1952.

These Lancashire fusiliers are on guard duty in Ismailia in the Canal Zone, October 1952.

General Mohamed Neguib greets Premier Aly Maher Pasha in Cairo, soon after the coup d'etat organised by Neguib which had the consequence of making Maher premier.

including about 100 police, surrendered and were disarmed. British casualties were three killed and thirteen wounded; the Ministry of the Interior estimated Egyptian losses at forty-six dead and over seventy injured.

Cairo responded the next day with riots. The police remained relatively inactive while attacks occurred first against British then against other foreign people and property. During the day many buildings were destroyed or damaged, including a British hotel, the British-owned Turf Club, the French Chamber of Commerce and the Swedish and Lebanese legations. There were sixty deaths, including the Canadian trade commissioner and prominent British residents. The Egyptian army was eventually called on to patrol the capital's streets.

King Farouk dismissed his prime minister Nahas Pasha for failing to maintain order. A series of administrations was formed over the next few months, but there was growing unrest in the country and the king continued to lose support. A *coup d'état* occurred on the night of 23 July under the direction of Major-General Mohammed Neguib, a popular figure with the military. A few days later King Farouk abdicated and his baby son Ahmed Fuad (born earlier that year) was proclaimed in his stead. Towards the end of the year the Egyptian Cabinet issued a decree conferring supreme powers on General Neguib for six months, backdated to the time of the coup. The 1923 constitution was abolished in December and Egypt became a republic in the following year. In the Canal Zone there was a falling-off of terrorist activity from February and the situation for the British continued to improve after Neguib's seizure of power.

THE KOREAN WAR

The People's Democratic Republic of Korea (North Korea) invaded the Republic of Korea (South Korea) on 25 June 1950, capturing Seoul a few days later. By January 1952 the war had been going on for thirty months and the Republic of Korea was now supported in its efforts to defeat the North (which was backed by the People's Republic of China) by seventeen other members of the United Nations, including Britain, Canada and the USA. Throughout the year the general line of the front, stabilised in November 1951, remained unchanged although there was some local fighting, mainly around important observation posts. In March, however, Chinese Communists accused American forces of using germ warfare and in June the American Air Force bombed hydro-electric plants in North Korea.

North Korea's Commander-in-Chief was its prime minister General Kim, while the forces for the South were under the UN. The 'unified command' in 1952 was held by General Matthew Ridgway until May when he was succeeded by General Mark Clark. Both were

General Ridgway (right) and General Eisenhower, wearing dark glasses, in Paris with René Pleven, the French Minister of National Defence, 29 May 1952.

American. By the end of 1952 there were some 538 British dead as a result of the war. This compared with 243 Canadians and over 22,000 Americans. Truce talks, which had begun in July 1951 between the United Nations and North Korea, had reached agreement on all but one matter (the repatriation of prisoners of war) by June 1952. But the armistice agreement was not to be signed until July 1953.

UNITED STATES OF AMERICA

America elected a new president in 1952. Harry Truman (Democrat), having served two terms, stood down. Adlai Stevenson was his party's nomination to succeed him. General Eisenhower was the Republican candidate, with Richard Nixon as his running mate. The 'I Like Ike' campaign reflected reality. Eisenhower's support translated into both a popular and electoral college majority. He had over six and a half million votes more than Stevenson and carried thirty-nine (442 votes) to nine states (89 votes). The Republicans also had a majority in the Senate and in the House of Representatives.

Eisenhower's success was partly attributed to the weakness of the Democrats in dealing with the 'Red menace'. Communism was greatly feared in mid-century America in the wake of the Soviet Union's postwar domination of Eastern Europe and the establishment of 'Red China' in 1949. This weakness was largely attributed to Communist sympathisers in the Truman administration. It was in this atmosphere that the Republican Senator Joseph McCarthy claimed in February 1950 that he knew the names of fifty-seven 'card-carrying Communists' in the State Department and that over 200 people employed there were known Communist sympathisers. The momentum was maintained thereafter, culminating in 1953 when McCarthy secured the chair of a Senate sub-committee to investigate 'un-American activities'.

Rarely is an American president accused of acting uncon-stitutionally. But this happened during 1952. In April members of the United Steel Workers announced their attention to hold a national strike for increased wages. But, given the importance of steel output for sustaining the war in Korea, Truman seized the steel industry to prevent this. The management sought injunctions against him and a Federal District Court ruled that the seizure was unconstitutional and that the steel plants should be returned to their owners. The strike began but was called off at the president's request, because the US Court of Appeals ruled that the plants should not yet be returned to the private sector. But on 2 June the Supreme Court itself ruled that Truman's seizure was unconstitutional. As a result the steel plants were reprivatised and a national strike began.

President Truman then asked Congress to pass a law permitting seizure in a national emergency. The Senate rejected the appeal and suggested using existing legislation. This the president rejected. The impasse was only solved by an agreement between management and labour worked out at the White House towards the end of the year.

The USA exploded a series of atomic bombs during the course of April 1952, the largest of which was greater than that dropped on Hiroshima or Nagasaki. The event was televised. The plane involved in the mission was flying at an altitude of 5 miles and the bomb exploded at between 3,000 and 3,500 feet above the ground. Some 1,500 troops were less than 4 miles from the target

America's biggest-ever atomic blast on 22 April 1952. Set off at Yucca Flat, Nevada, the pillar of smoke rose to a height of 35,000 feet above the desert.

area, taking shelter in 4-foot deep foxholes. Dark glasses were issued to the troops for added protection and the soldiers were encouraged to look away: the flash was estimated to be 175 times as powerful as the brilliance of the sun. No ill-effects were reported. Within two hours of the explosion paratroopers from the 82nd Airborne Division had landed on one side of the target area and moved across it to meet ground troops coming from the other side. The only discomfort was said to be caused by the clouds of dust.

FIRST STEPS TOWARDS EUROPEAN UNION

'We must build a kind of United States of Europe. . . . The first step . . . must be a partnership between France and Germany.' This was the heart of a speech given by Churchill at Zurich in September 1946. The call was to be acted upon within four years and would see the first tangible results in 1952. Each year since 1945, 8 May had been celebrated as the anniversary of the end of the Second World War in Europe. Significantly, Robert Schuman (the French foreign minister) chose 9 May 1950 to introduce the plan named after him for

---

Vittorio Emanuele ORLANDO   RIP 1952

Prime minister of Italy 1917–19 he led the Italian delegation to the Paris Peace Conference. He was the last of the 'Big Four' (Woodrow Wilson, Georges Clemenceau and David Lloyd-George), all of whom had died before 1952. Soon after Mussolini and the Fascists came to power in Italy he retired from public life (1925). He re-emerged after the liberation of Rome and played a leading part in Italian politics until his resignation over foreign policy matters in 1947.

European integration. He acknowledged that 'Europe will not be created all at once' but proposed that the combined coal and steel production (the materials which had fuelled war between these nations three times in under eighty years) of France and Germany should be placed under a common, supranational authority. He saw such a move as 'the first stage in a European federation'.

The European Coal and Steel Community was established under the Treaty of Paris which had been signed in 1951 and came into force on 25 July 1952. There were six signatories – France, Germany, Italy, Belgium, the Netherlands and Luxembourg. The UK was involved because although Churchill had been the first postwar leader to speak in terms of a united Europe, he maintained that Britain's interests lay in the Commonwealth and the 'special relationship' with the USA rather than in Europe. This continued to be the Conservative Party's policy on its return to power.

Recognising that personnel as much as materials made for war, another French prime minister, René Pleven, had urged a supranational European army in October 1950. This was after several European statesmen, including Churchill, had spoken in favour of a continental army earlier that year. Pleven proposed that within the suggested army there should be no specifically national unit larger than a battalion. A treaty to establish what was to be known as the European Defence Community (EDC) was signed in Paris on 27 May 1952 by the six countries which had entered the European Coal and Steel Community. The EDC was defined in the treaty as 'of supranational character with common institutions, common armed forces and a common budget'. Britain (Anthony Eden) and the USA (Dean Acheson) joined in a tripartite declaration with France that any threat to the EDC would be regarded as a threat to their own security.

The British government supported the venture but declined to join it because of overseas commitments. The French National Assembly did not ratify the treaty, and so the proposals for a European army effectively died for the remainder of the twentieth century.

1952: A Year to Remember

WEATHER

Perhaps the most memorable aspects of the weather in 1952 were the Lynmouth floods in August and the dense fog in the London area in early December. Otherwise (perhaps as always) the weather was variable. For much of the first quarter of the year it was often cold and snowy. There was a severe snowstorm and gale in the south-east on 29 March. But both April and May were sunny, with London reaching 79°F on 30 April and 86°F on 18 May. June was dull and changeable with higher than average rainfall in the west and north. Many places, especially in the south, had little rain for most of July, but August was disappointing with heavy rain in many places. Oxford had its coldest September since before the early nineteenth century. October was colder, sunnier and wetter than usual. The cold continued into November but was now accompanied by snow and sleet. Snowfall was heavier than in any November since 1919. December was the fourth consecutive cold month.

THE LYNMOUTH FLOOD DISASTER

The villages of Lynton and Lynmouth together exemplified all that made the Exmoor area so beautiful. They were the glory of north Devon and a favourite with honeymooners, at least since the poet Shelley came to stay at Lynmouth with his sixteen-year-old bride, far away from his family's disapproval, and extolled the place. But this seaside village, through which the River Lyn flows, was to be the scene of a sudden deluge that all too vividly demonstrated the destructive power of nature. Lynton, half a mile away on the hilltop almost vertically above Lynmouth, was to suffer too. A cliff railway, built from money provided by George Newnes (founder and publisher of *Tit Bits*) in 1890, connected the two villages.

In 1952 it was in fact two small rivers, the West Lyn and East Lyn, which converged in the middle of Lynmouth at a right angle to take

A man of seventy-five, Mr Worth, is given a piggyback rescue from his flooded home, 15 August 1952.

the rainwater draining from the heights of Exmoor into the harbour. During the holiday season on the night of Friday 15/Saturday 16 August some 9 inches of rain fell in the area, the highest and wettest part of Devon. This was equivalent to one-eighth of the average annual rainfall. Rivulets quickly formed and 250 square miles of flooding occurred. The explanation at the time was that a small thundery depression met a current of warm moist air in just the wrong place. Such was the power generated by this storm that it tore down cables, uprooted trees and 20-ton rocks in the river were, in the words of one local resident, 'chucked about like pebbles'.

One of the cars washed away by the force of the water during the Lynmouth flood disaster.

The rainfall was sudden, heavy and at night. People were in local public houses and on the streets as well as at home. It was around 7.45pm that the Lynmouth police learnt that the Simonsbath–Lynton road had been washed away. Soon after, the culvert at Ilkerton burst and so the fire service was mobilised too. The force of the water led the West Lyn to cut itself a new channel some 200 feet long to join the East Lyn – wiping out all that stood in its way, including a car park. Lynmouth was now split in two. On the west side the river was still running its normal course. It was, however, flooded and had risen 12 feet above the West Lyn Bridge.

People took refuge in the upper storeys of their homes. Soon even this was not enough for some as they ripped open roofs and clambered to safety over the tiles. Under these conditions, electricity supplies soon failed and trees, cars, caravans and people were swept out to sea. Roads, bridges, buildings, cars, coaches and boats all disappeared. There were cars in trees, trees in houses. The Red Cross, the St John Ambulance Brigade, the Women's Voluntary Service, the Royal Society for the Prevention of Cruelty to Animals (RSPCA) and others all came to the rescue. The Exeter RSPCA, making use of the Society's night ambulance which was immediately driven down from London, was able to rescue more than a hundred animals including dogs, cats, goats, fowls, ferrets, rabbits and goldfish. Not one single animal needed to be destroyed. The night ambulance also delivered dog and cat food and fowl meal to the flooded area.

There were tales of lucky human escapes too – sixty people were said to have been evacuated from a hotel roof by means of a ladder perched against a sill just 3 inches thick. But there were an estimated thirty-one fatalities, including the vice-president and vice-chairman of the Lynton and Lynmouth branch of the British Legion, and Mrs Emily Ridd, a descendant of the Ridds who feature in the novel *Lorna Doone*. Her grandson and two hitchhikers taking shelter were also killed. Residents, including sixty ex-service families, and holidaymakers were evacuated mainly to Lynton, Minehead and Barnstaple.

Few residents were insured against flooding and there was widespread damage to public services and communications. Around sixty houses and hotels had been destroyed and others needed to be demolished. The government, armed services and above all the public responded to the disaster. A flood relief fund was set up in the hope of raising £250,000. The government contributed £25,000 and there was a suggestion that a state lottery be set up to help the fund. Holiday towns organised collections, Butlin's Holiday Camps raised £500 and the post office allowed parcels to the stricken area to be sent free of charge. When the appeal closed, over £1.3 million had been received.

THE LONDON SMOG

A policeman wearing smog protection.

Fog and London had long been associated but the capital was to face its greatest attack in 1952. The 'peasouper' and Dickens's 'London particular' had entered the language as descriptions of the type of fog which arose from droplet formation around and mixture with pollution particles. It was also known as smog, a term coined from the words smoke and fog at the beginning of the twentieth century. But this only become a familiar term in the wake of 5–9 December 1952, the days when smog had the deadliest effect in London's history.

Wind, pollution, temperature distributions and humidity all govern variations in visibility. In meteorological terms, the smog in question arose through an anticyclone which had spread from the north-west at the beginning of December and became stationary over the Thames Valley. It was filled with a pool of cold stagnant air to a depth of between 200 and 500 feet, within which a fog was formed. Smoke from London's chimneys made the fog worse – and this of course was before clean air legislation.

It has been estimated that in the early 1950s, because of home consumption of coal, a thin fog hung over London for between forty and sixty days a year. Towards the end of the year around 70,000 tons of coal were burnt every day. In combination with other aspects of daily life in the capital, this meant that 1,000 tons of smoke particles, 2,000 tons of sulphur dioxide, 140 tons of hydrochloric acid and 14 tons of fluorine compounds were emitted daily. The imperfect combustion of coal and exhaust fumes from motor vehicles created 8,000 tons of carbon monoxide. The air in December 1952, however, contained about ten times the quantity of pollutants normal for the time of year, and the concentration of sulphur dioxide was particularly strong. This affected people's breathing. The incoming heat from burning coal, body heat and the winter sun is likely to have raised the temperature of the fog area by about 10°F. But the fog remained cold and the temperature below freezing. Atmospheric pollution had an important indirect effect on further reducing visibility. By providing an abundance of nuclei for the formation of water droplets, the pollution probably caused the droplets of the London fog to be smaller, more numerous and more stable than those of the fog over the surrounding countryside. This produced a denser and less easily cleared fog.

Londoners first encountered this particular fog on the morning of Friday 5 December. It was at its worst until the Monday and only really cleared on the following day. In the west Westminster, Kensington and Chelsea suffered. In the east it was Holborn and the City, while across the river Battersea, Lambeth and Southwark saw the worst of it. There were smaller concentrations along low-lying parts of the Thames and Lea Valleys.

The fog was dense, quick to form and slow to disperse. It reduced visibility to less than 20 yards and, on occasion, to less than 10 yards. This had an immediate and sustained effect on transport. Train services were greatly disrupted. Many journeys took longer and some services were cancelled. Air services were suspended and traffic on the river (still a busy artery through the capital at this time) halted. Saturday's sport was badly hit by frost and fog, with many matches having to be cancelled. Conditions indoors were often as bad. On 8 December at the Festival Hall, on the South Bank of the Thames, the fully lit balcony was invisible from the stage. Meanwhile many householders in the areas affected by the fog found an oily greasy film on indoor surfaces; despite strenuous efforts, this would invariably reappear within an hour of being wiped clean.

It was estimated that the fog of early December killed around four thousand people. According to one expert in 1953, the death rates in London as a result of this fog almost reached those of the cholera epidemic of nearly a hundred years earlier and the influenza epidemic immediately after the end of the First World War. In comparison with recent years, the mortality rate for newborn infants had almost doubled, while that for those aged between one and twelve months had more than doubled. Generally speaking, deaths of children had increased by one-third, those of young adults by almost two-thirds. Those aged forty-five and over, however, were the most seriously affected. Half the increase in the death rate was attributed to bronchitis (up from 76 to 704) or pneumonia (45 to 168). But it was also argued that the adverse weather had seen an increase in deaths from respiratory tuberculosis, cancer of the lung, coronary disease and influenza. Interestingly though, there was no increase in road accident deaths (there were after all few vehicles on the road and those that were travelled very slowly) or in suicides.

There were also animal casualties and this led to disputes among scientists as to the exact nature of the harmful ingredients of the fog. There were show cattle which had died as a result of the fog. These had had their straw changed very frequently. This was not so for sheep and pigs in nearby pens and they survived.

But more widely the seriousness of the fog and the related deaths led to increased agitation for legislation against unnecessary pollution of London's air. The Committee on Air Pollution under Sir Hugh Beaver was soon established and reported in 1955. Its recommendations led to the Clean Air Act of the following year. Furthermore the City of London introduced some control regulations in 1955. Those for Greater London began in 1958. The days of the 'London particular' were numbered and areas such as Camden and Canonbury, which partly because of the prevalence of fog there had previously had few middle-class residents, began to undergo social change.

THE HARROW & WEALDSTONE RAILWAY DISASTER

It was soon after 8.15am on Wednesday 8 October that a local passenger train travelling from Tring in Hertfordshire to London Euston crossed from the London-bound (Up) slow railway line to the Up fast railway line at Harrow & Wealdstone station. It then, as timetabled, stopped at the Up fast platform. This was to allow urban

commuter services priority over late running expresses from the north of the country. But even the local train was slightly late. There had been fog in the early morning but now that had almost cleared. Special fog procedures had ceased to operate less than 10 minutes before.

The local train comprised nine non-corridor coaches and was packed with 700 passengers. There were about 300 more waiting on the platform to board it. In order to speed things up and to help accommodate the extra passengers, the guard had allowed some people into the brake van. Having checked that everyone was indeed 'all aboard', he was walking back to his van to resume the journey to Euston. The train had been at the platform less than 2 minutes. Suddenly the sleeping-car express from Perth to Euston, travelling at between 55 and 60 mph, slammed into the rear of the local train. It should not have been on that part of the line but presumably as a result of the recent fog the driver had failed to notice (and had therefore passed) the signals. The express hit the stationary train with such force that the last three coaches of the latter were compressed into the space of just one coach. The locomotive of the

Rescue workers search the wreckage of the three-train crash for survivors, 8 October 1952. An official likened the scene to a battlefield.

express train eventually stopped, blocking the Down fast line 78 yards beyond the point of impact with the first three coaches piled up behind it.

The signalman at Harrow, Mr Armitage, although severely shocked, immediately threw all signals in the area to danger and sent out the 'obstruction danger' signal. But he was too late. Just before the accident had occurred, he had accepted the late running 8am Down express from Euston to Liverpool and Manchester. This express train of fifteen coaches was drawn by two engines, one of which was the newly modified and newly named *Princess Anne*. In order to make up time this express had made a rapid start from Euston and as it approached Harrow it was already travelling at 60 mph – a few seconds after the first collision.

Seeing the Perth–Euston express enter the station and fearing the worst, Mr Armitage had activated detonators on the Down line in the Harrow area. The driver of the Liverpool express responded immediately to the warning crack of the detonators by applying the emergency brake. But it was too late. The locomotives struck the engine of the derailed Perth express, mounted and crossed the Down fast platform and overturned, blocking the Up electric line from Watford. This cut off the traction current which stopped an approaching electric train and thus prevented a further catastrophe. The exact moment of the disaster was known because the vibrations of the initial collision had stopped the station's clocks. That on the platform showed eighteen and half minutes past eight while the one in the tower, being deliberately set a little fast to assist would-be passengers, was one minute later.

The three rear coaches of the Tring–Euston train, the front part of the Perth express and the seven coaches of the Liverpool express now constituted a compact mass of wreckage 45 yards long, 18 yards wide and 10 yards high between the station platforms. Underneath it all was the engine of the Perth train. About 112 people were killed instantly; 10 died later. Some 200 were injured. Casualties included the engine crew of the Perth express.

The first ambulance and doctor arrived within 3 minutes and the police and fire brigade were there soon afterwards. Although the risk of fire was quite great – the kitchen car of the Liverpool express had used gas cylinders and their valves had broken off – there were few incidents of fires breaking out. A 'tunnel' was constructed under the wreckage and the job of rescuing people, caring for the injured and carrying out the dead soon began. The local community, voluntary services, clergy and Salvation Army were among those who responded to these needs. Anne Lee, a student nurse aged fifteen, worked for twenty-two hours without a break. Then she collapsed, was taken to hospital and was initially thought to have been involved in the crash.

Also actively involved were the Americans. Colonel Eugene Coler, Chief Air Surgeon of the 7th Air Division of the United States Air Force, was at the Division's headquarters at nearby Ruislip. He arranged for doctors, nurses and orderlies to come straightaway to Harrow. He also arranged for supplies of blood plasma to be flown from Burtonwood air base in Lancashire.

There was understandably widespread media interest, including on this occasion BBC television. An outside broadcast unit, originally intended to go to the Ascot Races, reached the scene. The evening news programme carried live transmissions from the scene of the accident. The rescue efforts

The tangled wreckage of the Harrow and Wealdstone crash.

continued for three days, with arc lamps erected in order to allow work to go on though the night. It took two days before the last two coaches of the local train were reached. On the Sunday the repair gangs paused at noon for a private service of prayer which had been arranged by the widows of the driver and fireman of the Perth–London express.

An inquiry was held and concluded that because of the smoke, steam and low sun the driver of the express had relaxed his concentration for some unexplained reason and therefore had not seen the yellow signal. No blame was attached to the signalman.

The accident happened just at the time when the final decision had been reached on a standard safety system – the Automatic Warning System – for all lines in Britain. This was intended to reduce the chances of such accidents. Less than ten days later (17 October) a press conference was held at King's Cross to show and explain the system in the engine cab. However, while the accident removed the last financial barriers to its widespread installation, Lieutenant-Colonel G.R.S. Wilson, the Chief Inspecting Officer, in his report acknowledged that had the system been in place at the time of the Harrow disaster, it would have reduced the effects but would not necessarily have prevented it from happening. This was Britain's most serious peacetime railway disaster and the worst since the collapse of the Tay Bridge (1879). Only one other passenger was killed in an accident on Britain's railways in 1952.

'COMING OUT' IN 1952 – DEBUTANTES

For others, 1952 would be remembered as the year they 'came out': their first Season. The 'Season' at this time still played a central role in British high society life – and in the domestic fashion industry. Until almost the end of the decade (1958) the daughters of the aristocracy were formally presented to the monarch. This high-profile ceremony served to announce their entry (or debut) into the wider world. It introduced the young debutante (or 'deb') into high society and, it was hoped, would ideally enable her to find a suitable husband.

The Season ran from May to the end of July and formally opened with the private view of the Royal Academy Summer Exhibition. Other key social occasions included the Chelsea Flower Show, the Fourth of June at Eton and the Trooping of the Colour. Sporting events included the Royal Ascot race meeting, Wimbledon Lawn Tennis Championships and the Henley Regatta. Goodwood and Cowes Week marked the end of the Season. Garden parties, luncheons and

Norman Hartnell designs which would probably appeal to a deb's mother – but they were the last word in 1952.

1952: A YEAR TO REMEMBER

balls filled the intervening gaps. Queen Charlotte's Birthday Ball, a charity event to raise money for the hospital named after its patron (consort to George III), took place in May. It became an essential event in the debutantes' calendar in 1928 and was still a high point in 1952. It was held at Grosvenor House. The young ladies, all dressed in white, descended twin staircases to the march from Handel's *Judas Maccabeus*, and curtsied to a huge iced cake in honour of Queen Charlotte. As she was born in 1744, it was decorated with 208 candles.

The cost of launching a deb in the 1950s was between £2,000 and £10,000. A debutante's ball dress could be central to her success in the Season. Formal codes of etiquette required that designs had to be reasonably modest, accompanied by delicate jewellery, usually a necklet of fine pearls. The dresses were normally strapless or held up with shoe-string straps. Bodices were neatly fitted and skirts full. They would be trimmed with ingenue embroidery or pale, artificial flowers. A deb of 1952 described her presentation dress as 'the sort of thing a grandmother might wear . . . I must have looked about 100.' Debutantes were, however, beginning to break the code as far as hats were concerned. Certainly by this time, although hats were usually worn, they were small and elegant, topped perhaps by a spray or a sprig of artificial flowers.

COMING OUT IN 1952 – NEW WORDS

Language changes constantly. The birth year of new words or terms can sometimes be identified. Similarly their lifespan will vary according to political and social factors, as with the words that follow.

Among those gaining currency or additional meanings were 'to prune', 'to tighten' and 'to freeze': all of these were used extensively by the press to describe economic policy and in particular policy towards government expenditure as outlined in the Budget. 'Probe' began to acquire a military significance. Forming new words by combining existing ones was long established. 'Ration-book', 'pleasure-cruise' and 'holidaymaker' were only a few years old in 1952 while those deemed to be new for that year (and which have survived) included 'food supplement', 'investment loss', 'manning requirements', 'negotiating machinery', 'oven-cook' and 'pilot scheme'. From 'to save face' came 'face-saving'. The Korean War and technology added/popularised in this year 'airstrike', 'evacuation strip', 'fire-fight' and 'truce negotiator'.

In the USA, words entering the language were said to include 'running mate' and 'keynote speech'. Both of these were clearly linked to the presidential election. From fashion and entertainment came the 'ponytail', 'biopic' (a biographical film) and 'panellist'.

CHRISTMAS AND THE END OF 1952

Christmas Day fell on a Thursday in 1952. This meant, with three full working days before the celebration, together with the huge response to the Post Office's plea to 'Post Early for Christmas', everyone received their cards and presents on time. This included even those who only posted them on 24 December as there were still postal deliveries on Christmas Day.

It was a mild day in most of the country, and many were able to attend a morning church service. Westminster Abbey was full, and there were 2,000 worshippers at St Paul's Cathedral and twice that number at Westminster Cathedral. The royal family (apart from Queen Mary and Princess Anne) attended Sandringham parish church. Prince Charles was there for the first time.

Christmas dinner and tea were among the high points of the day, with chicken the single most popular dish. While most spent Christmas at home receiving or visiting family locally, people were becoming more mobile and there was some public transport to enable outside activities to take place. Football matches for instance might be played. But home entertainment or radio/television was

Elizabeth II makes the first Christmas Day radio broadcast of her reign, from Sandringham.

the recourse of most, with the queen's (live) broadcast at three minutes past three another high point. That time had been decided for the first such broadcast in 1932 as being the optimum for both the nation and Empire. As a feature it was not expected to outlive its founder, George V. Indeed, there was no such broadcast in the early years of George VI. But, re-established in wartime, it had continued thereafter.

Depending on listeners' interests, other radio broadcast highlights this day included a repeat of the *Lessons and Carols* service from King's College, Cambridge, which had first been heard the afternoon before, Billy Cotton, Wilfred Pickles and *Archie Andrews' Christmas Party*. Possibly during the Christmas meal itself there was a chance to listen (again) to one of the most celebrated ITMA shows. Dating from 1944, it had been recorded in front of the Home Fleet in Scapa Flow. In addition, listeners could tune in to *Twenty Questions* and music from the BBC Symphony Orchestra under Adrian Boult. The Home Service closed in seasonal style with a history of the robin.

Television programmes were shown for twelve hours from 11am – but with breaks. Children could look forward to *Andy Pandy* and *The Flowerpot Men* while for the adults there was a Laurel and Hardy film (*Swiss Miss*) made in 1938. This time the pair played two mousetrap salesmen in Switzerland (on the presumption that as that country had the most cheese it would have the most mice) who run into trouble with a cook, a gorilla and two opera singers. A more serious reminder of the world beyond the shores that day was *A Christmas Card from Korea*. Most Boxing Day television was devoted to racing and news although it did include Cicely Courtneidge in *Gay's the Word* by Ivor Novello.

Entertainment outside the home that Christmas included *Sleeping Beauty* on ice at the Empire Pool, Wembley. The grand finale included a mock-up of the BOAC Comet jet. *Dick Whittington* at the London Palladium included a cooking lesson by David Dale and Richard Hearne, while Slighty in *Peter Pan* at the Scala was played by Kenneth Williams.

New Year's Eve was very similar to that of the year before. This time the Chelsea Arts Ball, conscious that the coming year would see the coronation, took 'Happy and Glorious' as its theme. A huge backcloth depicted in brilliant colours the Lion and the Unicorn 'fighting for the crown'. In the centre of the dance floor was a medieval archway. At midnight, amid a massive release of balloons, a tinsel sculpture of a woman emerged to wild cheering. In less than six months all this would be for real.

INDEX